HENRY CISNEROS

HENRY CISNEROS

Christopher Henry

CHELSEA HOUSE PUBLISHERS

NEW YORK ■ PHILADELPHIA

CHELSEA HOUSE PUBLISHERS

Editorial Director: Richard Rennert
Executive Managing Editor: Karyn Gullen Browne
Copy Chief: Robin James
Picture Editor: Adrian G. Allen
Art Director: Robert Mitchell
Manufacturing Director: Gerald Levine

HISPANICS OF ACHIEVEMENT
Senior Editor: Philip Koslow

Staff for HENRY CISNEROS
Copy Editor: Catherine Iannone
Assistant Editor: Mary B. Sisson
Designer: M. Cambraia Magalhães
Picture Researcher: Villette Harris
Cover Illustrator: Alex Zwarenstein

First Printing

1 3 5 7 9 8 6 4 2

Library of Congress Cataloging-in-Publication Data
Henry, Christopher E.
Henry Cisneros / Christopher E. Henry
p. cm.—(Hispanics of achievement)
Includes bibliographical references (p.) and index.
0-7910-2019-3
0-7910-2020-7 (pbk.)
1. Cisneros, Henry—Juvenile literature. 2. Cabinet officers—United States—
Biography—Juvenile literature. 3. Mayors—Texas—Biography—Juvenile literature. 4.
Mexican Americans—Biography—Juvenile literature. I. Title. II. Series.
E840.8.C52H45 1994
976.4'351063'092—dc20
94-185
[B]
CIP
AC

CONTENTS

JOAN BAEZ
Mexican-American folksinger

RUBÉN BLADES
Panamanian lawyer and entertainer

JORGE LUIS BORGES
Argentine writer

PABLO CASALS
Spanish cellist and conductor

MIGUEL DE CERVANTES
Spanish writer

CESAR CHAVEZ
Mexican-American labor leader

JULIO CÉSAR CHÁVEZ
Mexican boxing champion

EL CID
Spanish military leader

HENRY CISNEROS
Mexican-American political leader

ROBERTO CLEMENTE
Puerto Rican baseball player

SALVADOR DALÍ
Spanish painter

PLÁCIDO DOMINGO
Spanish singer

GLORIA ESTEFAN
Cuban-American singer

GABRIEL GARCÍA MÁRQUEZ
Colombian writer

FRANCISCO JOSÉ DE GOYA
Spanish painter

JULIO IGLESIAS
Spanish singer

RAUL JULIA
Puerto Rican actor

FRIDA KAHLO
Mexican painter

JOSÉ MARTÍ
Cuban revolutionary and poet

RITA MORENO
Puerto Rican singer and actress

PABLO NERUDA
Chilean poet and diplomat

OCTAVIO PAZ
Mexican poet and critic

PABLO PICASSO
Spanish artist

ANTHONY QUINN
Mexican-American actor

DIEGO RIVERA
Mexican painter

LINDA RONSTADT
Mexican-American singer

ANTONIO LÓPEZ DE SANTA ANNA
Mexican general and politician

GEORGE SANTAYANA
Spanish philosopher and poet

JUNÍPERO SERRA
Spanish missionary and explorer

LEE TREVINO
Mexican-American golfer

PANCHO VILLA
Mexican revolutionary

CHELSEA HOUSE PUBLISHERS

HISPANICS OF ACHIEVEMENT

Rodolfo Cardona

The Spanish language and many other elements of Spanish culture are present in the United States today and have been since the country's earliest beginnings. Some of these elements have come directly from the Iberian Peninsula; others have come indirectly, by way of Mexico, the Caribbean basin, and the countries of Central and South America.

Spanish culture has influenced America in many subtle ways, and consequently many Americans remain relatively unaware of the extent of its impact. The vast majority of them recognize the influence of Spanish culture in America, but they often do not realize the great importance and long history of that influence. This is partly because Americans have tended to judge the Hispanic influence in the United States in statistical terms rather than to look closely at the ways in which individual Hispanics have profoundly affected American culture. For this reason, it is fitting that Americans obtain more than a passing acquaintance with the origins of these Spanish cultural elements and gain an understanding of how they have been woven into the fabric of American society.

It is well documented that Spanish seafarers were the first to explore and colonize many of the early territories of what is today called the United States of America. For this reason, stu-

7

dents of geography discover Hispanic names all over the map of
the United States. For instance, the Strait of Juan de Fuca was
named after the Spanish explorer who first navigated the waters
of the Pacific Northwest; the names of states such as Arizona (arid
zone), Montana (mountain), Florida (thus named because it was
reached on Easter Sunday, which in Spanish is called the feast of
Pascua Florida), and California (named after a fictitious land in
one of the first and probably the most popular among the Spanish
novels of chivalry, *Amadis of Gaul*) are all derived from Spanish;
and there are numerous mountains, rivers, canyons, towns, and
cities with Spanish names throughout the United States.

  Not only explorers but many other illustrious figures in
Spanish history have helped define American culture. For example, the 13th-century king of Spain, Alfonso X, also known as
the Learned, may be unknown to the majority of Americans, but
his work on the codification of Spanish law has greatly influenced
the evolution of American law, particularly in the jurisdictions of
the Southwest. For this contribution a statue of him stands in the
rotunda of the Capitol in Washington, D.C. Likewise, the name
Diego Rivera may be unfamiliar to most Americans, but this
Mexican painter influenced many American artists whose paintings, commissioned during the Great Depression and the New
Deal era of the 1930s, adorn the walls of government buildings
throughout the United States. In recent years the contributions of
Puerto Ricans, Mexicans, Mexican Americans (Chicanos), and
Cubans in American cities such as Boston, Chicago, Los Angeles,
Miami, Minneapolis, New York, and San Antonio have been
enormous.

  The importance of the Spanish language in this vast cultural
complex cannot be overstated. Spanish, after all, is second only to
English as the most widely spoken of Western languages within
the United States as well as in the entire world. The popularity of
the Spanish language in America has a long history.

  In addition to Spanish exploration of the New World, the
great Spanish literary tradition served as a vehicle for bringing the

language and culture to America. Interest in Spanish literature in America began when English immigrants brought with them translations of Spanish masterpieces of the Golden Age. As early as 1683, private libraries in Philadelphia and Boston contained copies of the first picaresque novel, *Lazarillo de Tormes*, translations of Francisco de Quevedo's *Los Sueños*, and copies of the immortal epic of reality and illusion *Don Quixote*, by the great Spanish writer Miguel de Cervantes. It would not be surprising if Cotton Mather, the arch-Puritan, read *Don Quixote* in its original Spanish, if only to enrich his vocabulary in preparation for his writing *La fe del cristiano en 24 artículos de la Institución de Cristo, enviada a los españoles para que abran sus ojos* (The Christian's Faith in 24 Articles of the Institution of Christ, Sent to the Spaniards to Open Their Eyes), published in Boston in 1699.

Over the years, Spanish authors and their works have had a vast influence on American literature—from Washington Irving, John Steinbeck, and Ernest Hemingway in the novel to Henry Wadsworth Longfellow and Archibald MacLeish in poetry. Such important American writers as James Fenimore Cooper, Edgar Allan Poe, Walt Whitman, Mark Twain, and Herman Melville all owe a sizable debt to the Spanish literary tradition. Some writers, such as Willa Cather and Maxwell Anderson, who explored Spanish themes they came into contact with in the American Southwest and Mexico, were influenced less directly but no less profoundly.

Important contributions to a knowledge of Spanish culture in the United States were also made by many lesser known individuals—teachers, publishers, historians, entrepreneurs, and others—with a love for Spanish culture. One of the most significant of these contributions was made by Abiel Smith, a Harvard College graduate of the class of 1764, when he bequeathed stock worth $20,000 to Harvard for the support of a professor of French and Spanish. By 1819 this endowment had produced enough income to appoint a professor, and the philologist and humanist George Ticknor became the first holder of the Abiel

Smith Chair, which was the very first endowed Chair at Harvard University. Other illustrious holders of the Smith Chair would include the poets Henry Wadsworth Longfellow and James Russell Lowell.

A highly respected teacher and scholar, Ticknor was also a collector of Spanish books, and as such he made a very special contribution to America's knowledge of Spanish culture. He was instrumental in amassing for Harvard libraries one of the first and most impressive collections of Spanish books in the United States. He also had a valuable personal collection of Spanish books and manuscripts, which he bequeathed to the Boston Public Library.

With the creation of the Abiel Smith Chair, Spanish language and literature courses became part of the curriculum at Harvard, which also went on to become the first American university to offer graduate studies in Romance languages. Other colleges and universities throughout the United States gradually followed Harvard's example, and today Spanish language and culture may be studied at most American institutions of higher learning.

No discussion of the Spanish influence in the United States, however brief, would be complete without a mention of the Spanish influence on art. Important American artists such as John Singer Sargent, James A. M. Whistler, Thomas Eakins, and Mary Cassatt all explored Spanish subjects and experimented with Spanish techniques. Virtually every serious American artist living today has studied the work of the Spanish masters as well as the great 20th-century Spanish painters Salvador Dalí, Joan Miró, and Pablo Picasso.

The most pervasive Spanish influence in America, however, has probably been in music. Compositions such as Leonard Bernstein's *West Side Story*, the Latinization of William Shakespeare's *Romeo and Juliet* set in New York's Puerto Rican quarter, and Aaron Copland's *Salon Mexico* are two obvious examples. In general, one can hear the influence of Latin rhythms—from tango to mambo, from guaracha to salsa—in virtually every form of American music.

This series of biographies, which Chelsea House has published under the general title HISPANICS OF ACHIEVEMENT, constitutes further recognition of—and a renewed effort to bring forth to the consciousness of America's young people—the contributions that Hispanic people have made not only in the United States but throughout the civilized world. The men and women who are featured in this series have attained a high level of accomplishment in their respective fields of endeavor and have made a permanent mark on American society.

The title of this series must be understood in its broadest possible sense: The term *Hispanics* is intended to include Spaniards, Spanish Americans, and individuals from many countries whose language and culture have either direct or indirect Spanish origins. The names of many of the people included in this series will be immediately familiar; others will be less recognizable. All, however, have attained recognition within their own countries, and often their fame has transcended their borders.

The series HISPANICS OF ACHIEVEMENT thus addresses the attainments and struggles of Hispanic people in the United States and seeks to tell the stories of individuals whose personal and professional lives in some way reflect the larger Hispanic experience. These stories are exemplary of what human beings can accomplish, often against daunting odds and by extraordinary personal sacrifice, where there is conviction and determination. Fray Junípero Serra, the 18th-century Spanish Franciscan missionary, is one such individual. Although in very poor health, he devoted the last 15 years of his life to the foundation of missions throughout California—then a mostly unsettled expanse of land—in an effort to bring a better life to Native Americans through the cultivation of crafts and animal husbandry. An example from recent times, the Mexican-American labor leader Cesar Chavez battled bitter opposition and made untold personal sacrifices in his effort to help poor agricultural workers who have been exploited for decades on farms throughout the Southwest.

The talent with which each one of these men and women may have been endowed required dedication and hard work to develop and become fully realized. Many of them have enjoyed rewards for their efforts during their own lifetime, whereas others have died poor and unrecognized. For some it took a long time to achieve their goals, for others success came at an early age, and for still others the struggle continues. All of them, however, stand out as people whose lives have made a difference, whose achievements we need to recognize today and should continue to honor in the future.

HENRY CISNEROS

CHAPTER

ONE

SHOWDOWN AT VIDOR

On September 14, 1993, a tall, dark-haired man in his mid-forties confronted a battery of microphones and tape recorders in a U.S. government office near the town of Vidor, Texas. Addressing the reporters massed in front of him, he explained why he had come back to his home state from his office in Washington, D.C. "We are here in east Texas to correct a wrong," he declared, "to help the people here reclaim their basic freedoms as citizens of the United States of America."

These words did not come from a hotheaded political agitator. They were uttered instead by a well-dressed government official, a man who had recently enjoyed a successful career in the financial industry and usually occupied a spacious office in the nation's capital, far removed from the sun-baked plains of east Texas. Henry G. Cisneros, secretary of housing and urban development in the administration of President Bill Clinton, was about to demonstrate that he was not only capable of running a government agency and managing a budget. He was about to reveal himself as a man of principle who was willing and able to fight for his ideals.

At the time of Cisneros's news conference, almost 30 years had passed since another Texan, President Lyndon B. Johnson, signed the 1964 Civil Rights Act,

Henry Cisneros, photographed outside the Alamo, in his native city of San Antonio, Texas. During his four highly effective terms as mayor of San Antonio during the 1980s, Cisneros emerged as the leading Hispanic political figure in the United States.

15

outlawing discrimination based on race, religion, or ethnic origin. But in September 1993, poor blacks in some Texas communities still found it difficult to make homes for their families. Even in those cases where both money for rent and public housing were available to them, African Americans in the state of Texas often discovered that they were still not accepted by their white neighbors.

Texas was certainly not the only state where housing discrimination continued long after federal laws prohibited such practices. In almost every state in the country, black Americans often discovered that there was an enormous difference between choosing a home and being allowed to live in that home. Racial discrimination by sellers, landlords, real estate agents, banks, and other institutions that provided financing was so much a part of American life that blacks found themselves—even in 1993—unable to purchase or rent homes in hundreds of communities and neighborhoods across the United States.

Vidor is a small town in east Texas with a dwindling population and an economy that offers little incentive for growth. Almost all of Vidor's nearly 11,000 residents are white, and some of them are poor. Poor whites are not unique to Vidor; hundreds of communities in east Texas, a major oil-producing region, were devastated during the 1980s when the price of oil went down on the world market.

Federal funds—representing the taxes paid by Americans of all races—were used to build public housing projects in Vidor and scores of other communities in east Texas. Vidor Village was a complex of 74 apartments that the U.S. government built in the town to help its poor residents enjoy decent living conditions. All these projects are overseen by Cisneros's agency, the Department of Housing and Urban Development (HUD).

Many of the nation's publicly financed housing projects, including Vidor Village, were from the beginning as racially segregated as the towns in which they were located. Over the years, the federal government has taken action to prohibit this unlawful discrimination. In February 1993, black tenants began to move into Vidor Village under the protection of a federal court's desegregation order.

In a six-month period, nine African Americans moved into Vidor Village. They included an elderly disabled man who lived alone, a single mother with three dependent children, another single mother with two children, and a man in his thirties who had been homeless before moving into the complex. Like their white neighbors, these tenants were poor; all they wanted from Vidor Village was a safe and affordable place to live.

The new black residents of Vidor Village were all forced to leave within six months. Some fled in terror after only a few weeks. Each of them had been harassed by some of Vidor Village's white residents, and some were threatened with physical violence. One of the black residents, Bill Simpson, told law enforcement authorities that whites in Vidor had threatened to lynch him. Simpson fled from Vidor Village— where he should have been as safe as any other U.S. citizen in his or her home. Ironically, he was shot dead days later in an unrelated incident in Beaumont, Texas, about 10 miles from Vidor.

When the national news media reported Bill Simpson's story, most Americans were outraged. They were shocked to discover that three decades after the passage of the 1964 Civil Rights Act, and a quarter-century after the Reverend Martin Luther King, Jr., had been assassinated while fighting for civil rights, a black man like Bill Simpson could not live peacefully in a housing project which had been paid for by their tax dollars. The outrage cut across party lines, political ideology, race, religion, and gender. Public opinion demanded that the Clinton administration, which identified itself with the fight for social justice, take swift and decisive action.

   After his election in November 1992, Clinton had asked Henry G. Cisneros, the former mayor of San Antonio, Texas, to become his secretary of housing and urban development. Like Lyndon Johnson, Cisneros was a lifelong Texan who had been interested in government and politics since his youth. Cisneros had been elected to San Antonio's city council at the age

Flanked by President Bill Clinton and Vice-President Al Gore, Cisneros speaks at a December 1992 news conference marking his appointment as secretary of housing and urban development. Shortly after taking office, Cisneros announced that one of his main priorities would be helping the homeless people of the nation's cities.

of 27 and had become its mayor when he was only 33 years old. He joined the Clinton administration shortly after the new president's inauguration in January 1993.

President Clinton met with Secretary Cisneros about a week after Bill Simpson was gunned down in Beaumont, Texas. Clinton was not sure how to handle the problem, but both he and Cisneros wanted to do something dramatic, something to demonstrate that the Clinton administration would be more vigorous than the previous administrations in fighting all types of discrimination.

Cisneros knew from personal experience what the people of Texas were like. An American of Mexican descent, the son of immigrants, Cisneros was well aware of the racism that survived in many parts of Texas, a racism directed against Mexicans and Mexican Americans as well as blacks. But Cisneros also knew that most Texans were fair and decent people, and he was confident that he would be able to reach those Texans and let them know that the government in Washington would stand behind them.

On September 14, 1993, Secretary Cisneros returned home to Texas to bring the power of the federal government to bear on Vidor Village, and by extension the nearly 200 federal housing projects in east Texas. Speaking at his news conference, he invoked the memory of Reverend Martin Luther King, Jr., stating, "Dr. King reminded us that each of us has an inalienable right to be safe and secure in our own home, free to live and move about unrestricted by intimidation and threats of violence, free to associate with people of any race, religion or cultural heritage. . . . In east Texas, there are hatemongers and racists who deny these basic rights to African Americans, Hispanics and other minorities. Despite the best efforts of the decent people of Vidor—the vast majority of people here—who have worked to create a healthy, harmonious environment, bigots and racists have poisoned the community with their ignorant prejudice."

Describing in detail the indignities and intimidations suffered by the black residents of Vidor Village during their brief tenancies, Cisneros got to the heart of the reason for his visit. He had not come to Vidor just to make a speech, or to condemn racism, or to offer moral support for the oppressed. He had come to Vidor to solve a problem, and would waste no time in doing so. "This entire effort represents a new direction for the department," he told the reporters. "Over the past 12 years, HUD's response [to discrimination] has been weak, inadequate and unsuccessful. . . . We are going to work with the good people of Vidor to make their public housing a source of community pride, and we're going to be here as long as it takes to make things right."

Cisneros then announced that he had asked for the resignations of the board of commissioners and the director of the Orange County Housing Authority, which managed Vidor Village, stating that they had "failed their responsibility to create a safe and secure environment for all people." In order to ensure that federal civil rights laws were carried out, he placed Vidor Village and three other federal housing projects in the area under the direct control and supervision of the Department of Housing and Urban Development.

Cisneros issued a thinly veiled warning to any whites in Vidor who might feel tempted to renew their harassment of future black tenants. He stated: "Associate Attorney General Webster L. Hubbell of the Justice Department is here as part of this coordinated effort. The U.S. Marshals Service, the FBI, and a staff of Justice Department lawyers will be working with us to facilitate the desegregation effort."

Cisneros made it clear that the Department of Housing and Urban Development fully intended to integrate Vidor Village. He predicted that a dozen black families would be the minimum number necessary to accomplish the plan.

The confrontation at Vidor Village provided Cisneros with a major, and early, victory in his new role as a federal official. Cisneros's political career had been

The headquarters of the U.S. Department of Housing and Urban Development (HUD), located in Washington, D.C. During the 1980s, HUD had been considered a stodgy and timid agency; in the 1993 Vidor Village controversy, Secretary Cisneros made it clear that his department was going to play an aggressive role in improving public housing.

built upon such confrontations; his election to the San Antonio City Council almost two decades earlier had come as the result of Mexican-American political empowerment. But Cisneros had not achieved success by being divisive or making capital out of racial antagonisms. He had proved during his four terms as San Antonio's mayor that he cared about—and respected—all people.

A month after he removed the local housing authority, Cisneros's observation regarding the decency of the overwhelming majority of Vidor's residents was underscored during a demonstration there. A white supremacist organization calling itself the Nationalist Movement announced that it would hold a march and rally in Vidor to celebrate the fact that blacks had been prevented from living peacefully in Vidor Village. The group applied for and received the necessary permit from Vidor's city government. The government had no alternative because the U.S. Constitution guarantees all citizens the rights of free speech and assembly.

Many of Vidor's residents, already angry at the way their town had been portrayed in the national media, were further riled by the news of the impending demonstration. Extra law enforcement officers— more than 100 of them—were brought into Vidor on the day of the march to bolster the local police force and the various federal agents who had been sent there at Cisneros's request.

The "demonstration" consisted of 13 marchers who wandered aimlessly through downtown Vidor under police protection, while several hundred protestors jeered and laughed at them. The marchers were not from Vidor, and the people of Vidor showed little sympathy with their presence. The fact that they were vastly outnumbered by those opposed to racial discrimination made it abundantly clear that Cisneros had been correct in his assessment of Vidor's population. Most important, the only "loser" in Vidor was racism itself. Neither Vidor's white population nor its local government were penalized in any manner.

Cisneros's decisive action in Vidor drew national acclaim. An editorial in the *New York Times* called his hands-on approach to housing integration "deeply gratifying." President Clinton and members of the cabinet understood that the new man at HUD had the toughness and intelligence to tackle difficult problems for the administration in the future.

No one who had followed Cisneros's political career was surprised by his performance in Vidor. During his tenure as mayor of San Antonio, he had been one of the rising young stars of American politics. Acclaimed as the most important and appealing Hispanic politician in the nation, Cisneros was often spoken of as a man with an unlimited future. But in 1989, family tragedy and a public scandal had caused him to abandon his political career. In the eyes of many observers, Cisneros could no longer be a factor in the life of the nation.

But Cisneros had quickly surmounted his personal difficulties. Given a new opportunity by President Clinton, Cisneros had come roaring back onto the national scene. And he had done it in the most appropriate way, by striking a blow for justice and tolerance in the state that had shaped his identity.

Coronado and His Captains, *by the contemporary New Mexican artist Gerald Cassidy, depicts the 16th-century Spanish explorer Francisco Vásquez de Coronado. During the 16th century, Coronado and other bold adventurers established the culture of Spain in the region that is now the state of Texas.*

STARTING OUT
IN TEXAS

When Henry Gabriel Cisneros was born in San Antonio, Texas, on June 11, 1947, his native state had been the scene of cultural conflict for more than 400 years. That conflict had begun in 1528, when a Spanish explorer named Álvar Núñez Cabeza de Vaca and three other hapless sailors swam to a shore along the Gulf of Mexico. The quartet were the sole survivors of a shipwreck. Decades later, after Cabeza de Vaca made his way back to Spain, he recorded his experiences, and thus began the history of the land that would one day be called Texas.

Long before Cabeza de Vaca and his comrades had been washed up along the Gulf Coast, Texas was home to another population—the Indians who had lived there for thousands of years. The needs and desires of the two groups—one wishing to preserve their traditional way of life, the other eager for wealth and glory—were bound to clash.

By about 1550, other Spanish explorers, led by Francisco Vásquez de Coronado, returned to Texas. They had not come there out of curiosity but rather out of greed. Stories of whole cities built of gold and diamonds lured the early explorers from Europe, who came to the new world to plunder and to conquer. The first confrontations between the native population and the European explorers were, more

often than not, marked by bloodshed, hatred, and
destruction.

More than a century elapsed before the first permanent Spanish settlement was established in Texas,
near the present-day city of El Paso, in 1682; other
Spanish settlements quickly followed. France also
took an interest in colonizing the huge land mass, but
neither the French nor the Spanish were able to
endure the continuous onslaught of Indian attacks. By
1700, most of the European settlements had been
abandoned. Spain still claimed ownership of the territory, however, typically disregarding any ownership
rights of the Indians who actually lived there.

Gradually, the Spanish reestablished their settlements and solidified their control over Texas.
The region's population rose gradually until 1800, at
which time as many as 10,000 Spanish settlers may
have been living in Texas. The region did not have
a government of its own; it was part of the Spanish colony of Mexico, which extended so far to the
north that it included most of the present-day state of
California.

As the Spanish colonists in Mexico intermarried
with the native Indian population, a new people came
into being. Though they spoke the Spanish language
and belonged to the Catholic church, the colony's
growing population also took many ideas and atti-
tudes from the rich culture of the Indians. They considered themselves Mexicans rather than Spaniards,
and early in the 19th century they revolted against
Spanish rule. Mexico gained its independence in 1821
and became a republic in 1823.

As Mexico established itself as an independent
nation, the United States, which had gained its independence from Great Britain in 1789, was also growing rapidly. U.S. citizens were pouring into Texas,
colonizing land that was rapidly being sold to them by

the new Mexican government. By 1836, there were about 30,000 Americans living in Texas, and they outnumbered the Mexicans four to one. Still, they lived under Mexican rule—their rights were property rights only, and did not include the right to sovereignty or self-government. These were terms that the Americans voluntarily accepted when they bought their land.

In some ways, the laws of Mexico were more humane than the laws of the United States, where slavery was still legal. Many of the American colonists brought their black slaves with them to Texas, and Mexico outlawed slavery as a result, although Mexico was incapable of fully enforcing its laws. The new Mexican government was extremely unstable, and

A map showing the Mexican states of Coahuila and Texas as they existed in 1833, 12 years after Mexico won its independence from Spain. In 1835, however, U.S. citizens in Texas took up arms against the Mexican government, determined to join their territory to the expanding United States.

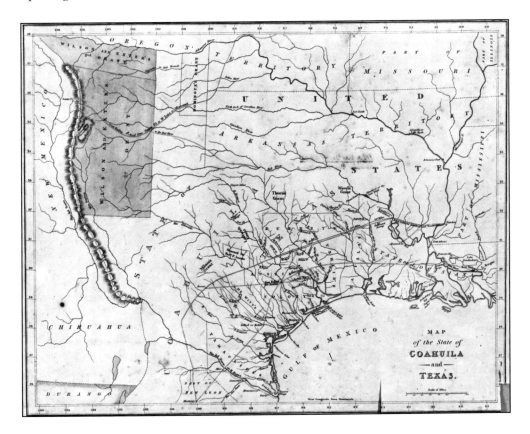

leadership changed hands frequently in the first few decades of its existence. Taking advantage of this situation, the American colonists in Texas became more and more difficult to govern.

The first major battle between the Mexicans and the American colonists occurred in October 1835, near Gonzáles. The colonists were victorious, and one month later, they set up their own provisional government. In December 1835, the Americans attacked the Mexicans at a town called San Antonio de Bexar, which is now San Antonio. Again, the Americans were victorious, and the contingent of Mexican soldiers that had been stationed at San Antonio de Bexar agreed to withdraw from the region and return to the area of Mexico south of the Rio Grande. During the battle, the Americans captured a Mexican fort known as the Alamo, which has often been inaccurately portrayed in movies and popular American mythology. Contrary to its Hollywood interpretation, the Alamo was not a massive fortress guarded by 30-foot-high walls. It was simply a collection of buildings, protected only by walls that were scarcely as high as a one-story building.

The defeated Mexican soldiers kept their word—after a fashion. They withdrew across the Rio Grande, but only temporarily. Two months later, they returned with heavy reinforcements, under the command of Antonio López de Santa Anna—Mexico's dictatorial ruler and leading general. The Mexican siege of the Alamo began on February 23, 1836. Defending the modest military installation were 150 Americans, including some who became famous in American folklore.

Among those at the Alamo was the legendary frontiersman Davy Crockett. The 50-year-old Crockett had fought against the Creek Indians a quarter-century earlier, but contrary to myth, he was always more of a politician than a warrior. He had been elected to the Tennessee legislature in 1821, and to the United States House of Representatives in 1827. However, he had lost his last congressional election in 1835. Apparently having nothing more interesting to do, he headed for Texas immediately after his defeat.

James Bowie, purported to have been the inventor of the bowie knife, was another of the Alamo's defenders. How and why Bowie became an American hero is perplexing. He and two of his brothers were slave traders, and Bowie's only interest in Texas appears to have been his desire to grab as much land as possible. Bowie befriended a high Mexican official in San Antonio de Bexar and married the man's daughter in 1831, obtaining a vast amount of land as his dowry. Five years later, Bowie showed his appreciation to his father-in-law by participating in the American revolt.

Removed from the romantic trappings of mythology, the American uprising in Texas that culminated in the siege of the Alamo was not a fight for freedom. It was all about land and money, and one of the "rights" that the settlers wanted was the ability to own slaves in Texas. The Americans had made an agreement with the Mexicans when they purchased their land grants; now the Americans had broken their agreement and were attempting to expel the Mexicans from part of their own country with armed force.

Ten days after the siege began, 4,000 Mexican soldiers surrounded the Alamo, outnumbering the defenders by more than 20 to 1. (Thirty-two more Americans had managed to slip through the Mexican lines and join the defenders.) Santa Anna demanded that the Americans surrender, but they refused to do so, perhaps out of sheer courage, but more likely because they knew they would be killed by Santa Anna's troops in any case.

James Bowie, credited with inventing the bowie knife, was among the 180 Americans defending the Alamo against a vastly superior force of Mexican troops in March 1836. After the Mexicans wiped out the defenders, Bowie and his companions were enshrined in American legend.

On March 6, 1836, the Mexicans attacked the Alamo from all sides. The fighting was ferocious, and the battle raged for hours. The greatest slaughter went on outside the walls as Santa Anna's men raced across open ground and were cut down en masse by the Alamo's defenders. No one knows how many Mexicans were killed at the Alamo, but estimates generally range from a minimum of 1,000 to as many as 2,000. But for the 180 or so men trapped inside the fort, the number of Mexican casualties was unimportant. As the Texans were killed and wounded, they could no longer defend the entire perimeter of the Alamo, and the surviving Mexicans, furious with a desire for vengeance, broke through. Inside the walls, the fighting became more vicious still—a virtual caldron filled with smoke, gunfire, screams, and the clash of bayonets and hunting knives. The bloodbath continued for hours, until only a handful of Texans remained alive.

What happened next has been the source of great disagreement among historians for more than a century and a half. Some say that all of the Alamo's defenders were eventually killed during the battle. Other accounts describe the taking of prisoners who were first tortured and then killed days later. But historians do agree on one point: there were no American survivors at the Alamo.

"Remember the Alamo" became the rallying cry of the Americans in Texas as they quickly moved to avenge the defeat at the Alamo and a later massacre at the town of Goliad only 13 days later, when Colonel James W. Fannin and 300 of his troops were executed by Santa Anna after surrendering. On April 21, General Sam Houston and a force of 800 Americans ambushed the remains of Santa Anna's army—which then numbered about 1,500—during their afternoon siesta. Houston's surprise attack proved to be one of the most spectacular victories in U.S. military history. Houston's men killed more than 600 Mexicans in less than 20 minutes; the rest, including Santa Anna, were captured. Only nine Americans were killed in the confrontation.

During the fighting in the spring of 1836, the Texans declared themselves to be an independent republic. Tensions with Mexico continued, and in 1845, the United States annexed Texas and granted the territory statehood. The loss of Texas was a blow to Mexico, but worse was in store. Under the slogan of Manifest Destiny, an expansionist fever gripped the United States. The administration of President James K. Polk set its sights on the remainder of Mexico's northern territories. In 1846, Polk sent 3,000 troops

to the Rio Grande to provoke a confrontation with the Mexicans; when the Mexicans fired at the Americans, the United States launched a full-scale invasion that resulted in the capture of Mexico City. Many Americans—among them future presidents Abraham Lincoln and Ulysses S. Grant—condemned the Mexican War of 1846–47 as a cowardly and unjust action, but there was no way of stemming the expansionist tide. The Treaty of Guadalupe Hidalgo, which ended the hostilities, deprived Mexico of a huge chunk of territory that included the present-day states of California, Arizona, New Mexico, Utah, Nevada, and Colorado.

For years to come, hatred and distrust marked the relations between Texans and the Mexicans from whom the land had been taken. As the events leading up to and following the battles at the Alamo were mythologized and distorted, each side became more inflexible.

The siege of the Alamo, depicted here in a painting by Harry A. McCardle, was a frightful bloodbath that cost the lives of at least 1,000 Mexican soldiers. After the battle, "Remember the Alamo" became a rallying cry for Texans in their drive for independence.

They were separated not only by the legacy of bloody warfare but also by language, culture, and race.

When the U.S. Civil War erupted in 1860, Texas seceded from the Union and became part of the Confederacy. Texas was far removed from most of the fighting, but the state sent many of its men to die on the battlefields. Despite the defeat of the Confederacy in 1865, Texas continued to grow and prosper. Its population at the beginning of the Civil War had been around 600,000; by the end of the 19th century, though, more than 3 million people lived in Texas, making it one of the nation's most populous states.

The mythology surrounding the battle at the Alamo has colored the way Americans view Texas history and the Texans themselves. Texas is often shrouded in images of the old West that—if they were ever a reality to begin with—have long ceased to have any relevance to the state today. Texas once was a primarily rural state, its economy dependent upon cotton farming and cattle ranching, but that changed more than a half-century ago, as industry began to dominate the economy and the population of cities such as Dallas and Houston expanded rapidly.

Until Alaska was granted statehood in 1959, Texas reigned as the nation's largest state in geographical area. Its 267,000 square miles create a vast expanse of land—so vast that at any given time the weather in different parts of the state can range from sunshine and blistering heat to bitter cold and snow. Texas shares a border with Mexico of about 1,000 miles, with the two nations separated by the Rio Grande. Bordered on the east by Louisiana and Arkansas, on the north by Oklahoma, and on the west by New Mexico, Texas is surrounded by a culturally and geographically diverse area.

During the 1990s, the population of Texas has continued to grow so rapidly that it is on the verge of replacing New York as the second most populous state, after California. Of the nearly 18 million people now residing in Texas, an estimated 25 percent are of Hispanic ancestry. Not surprisingly, almost the entire Hispanic population of the state—whether recent immigrants or long-established native Texans— derives from Mexico.

Although Henry Cisneros is a native Texan who grew up in the comfort of a modern home in a pleasant suburb of San Antonio, he was profoundly influenced from earliest childhood by the saga of his Mexican grandfather.

José Rómulo Munguía y Torres was born in Guadalajara, Mexico, in 1882. From the very beginning, his life was a bitter and desperate struggle. An orphan at the age of eight in a society hardened to the sufferings of the impoverished—of which there were many—he went to work in order to earn his daily bread. Barely surviving on the few centavos he was paid for menial chores, the boy sought another form of compensation—knowledge. Knowledge, he discovered, was free to those who listened, observed, and studied. Even a poor boy could gain knowledge, and someday, he could use that knowledge to provide for other needs.

The orphan eventually found a job as a printer's helper, and he greatly enjoyed the work despite his arduous duties. Filthy with printer's ink, his arms and legs covered with scratches and bruises from the heavy bars of type and the clanking presses, José Rómulo gradually learned a trade. Combined with the learning he was acquiring, his practical ability was a valuable asset. But his new knowledge soon got him into more trouble than he had originally bargained for.

As a teenager, José Rómulo left Guadalajara and moved to Mexico City. There, he took a job with a newspaper owned by a family who opposed the cur-

As depicted in a 19th-century painting, Mexican forces surrender to U.S. general Sam Houston after the Battle of San Jacinto in 1836. Ten years later, the United States launched an all-out war against Mexico and annexed half the territory of its southern neighbor.

rent Mexican president, Porfirio Díaz. Díaz had gained the presidency in 1877 and had set out to modernize the economy of Mexico. Unfortunately for most Mexicans, Díaz tried to accomplish this goal by helping the rich at the expense of the poor. He invited foreign business interests to exploit Mexico's natural resources, and he took land away from Mexico's peasants in order to set up large estates for wealthy landowners. The economy began to prosper, but very few Mexicans benefited from the change. At the same time, Díaz ruled the country as a dictator, tolerating no opposition to his policies. He created a special police force called the Rurales to control the countryside; the Rurales routinely terrorized the peasants and arrested anyone who spoke out against the Díaz regime. As the 19th century came to an end, however, opposition to Díaz continued to grow, as Mexican men and women committed themselves to overthrowing Díaz, even if it cost them their lives.

As opposition grew, Díaz decided to silence those newspapers that were criticizing his policies. One night, when José Rómulo Munguía, now 20 years old, was working at the newspaper office, Díaz's police surrounded the building and arrested everyone inside. Munguía was dragged before a magistrate and sentenced to death for treason, without even the pretense of a trial.

As he remained in jail awaiting his execution, Munguía resolved that he would not walk quietly before a firing squad and accept death. The orphan who had survived the streets of Guadalajara, who had lived hand-to-mouth for years after the death of his

Porfirio Díaz (1830–1915) served as president of Mexico for almost the entire period between 1877 and 1911. Though Díaz modernized Mexico's economy, he oppressed the poor and terrorized political opponents. His policies eventually sparked the Mexican Revolution of 1910.

parents, would not now, after all that long struggle, surrender to the tyrant Díaz. If he had to die, he would die fighting for his freedom. Munguía carefully planned a daring escape from his captors, but it proved not to be necessary. President Díaz suddenly commuted Munguía's death sentence and set him free.

Díaz was not being merciful—only cunning. The Mexican president had the good sense to understand that making martyrs of young journalists would only strengthen the resolve of those against him. Díaz's supposed change of heart certainly did not fool Munguía either; his experience only reinforced his principles and his strong belief that Díaz had to be removed. Munguía would, in fact, outlive the tyrannical Mexican president by many decades.

The Mexican Revolution began in 1910, when Francisco Indalécio Madero spearheaded a broad-based challenge to the Díaz regime. Aided by the military exploits of the peasant leader Emiliano Zapata in southern Mexico, and of the former bandit Pancho Villa in the north, Madero forced Díaz to resign the presidency in May 1911. Díaz died in exile in Paris, France, in 1915.

Unfortunately, the fall of Díaz did not bring peace to Mexico. Following the assassination of Madero, the revolution raged on for another 10 years, as various factions struggled to control the nation. Finally, Mexico achieved a measure of stability in 1920, when General Álvaro Obregón became president and began a program of reform. Before long, however, Mexico was subjected to a series of corrupt and brutal governments controlled by the political machine of another former general, Plutarco Elías Calles.

José Rómulo Munguía, the printer's apprentice turned revolutionary, had lived through 10 years of bloody revolution only to find that in the mid-1920s, Mexico was again becoming a nation in which a man might be imprisoned or even put to death simply for stating beliefs that displeased the government.

In 1926, only three years before the stock market crash that plunged the United States into a desperate economic crisis, Munguía decided that he had had enough of revolutionary politics for the time being. He was then 44 years old, with a wife and children. Neither his philosophy nor his commitment to justice had changed, but like so many other potential immigrants from all corners of the earth, his greatest desire was to provide a homeland for his children—and for his family's future generations—that would be free from fear and oppression. He looked toward the north, across the Rio Grande.

Though Munguía was aware that the United States had habitually taken advantage of Mexico, he also knew that Americans lived under a true democratic republic—one that had been founded upon a constitution guaranteeing the rights of citizens to freedom of speech and assembly. Thus the United States, for all its reputation as an overbearing neighbor, offered great hope to Munguía and his compatriots, who began to flee Mexico in droves as the political situation under the Calles regime became increasingly unstable.

While immigrants from nations such as China, Russia, Ireland, and Italy had to endure long voyages through treacherous seas in order to reach the United States, the journey for the Munguía family was much simpler. For them, freedom and stability awaited just across the river in Texas. During the 1920s, the U.S. government was not deeply concerned about immigration from Mexico. In the years to come, however, the Rio Grande would come to have increasing political significance. Immigration would become a source of great controversy, as U.S. officials worked to hold back the hundreds of thousands of Mexicans

Government troops fire upon rebels led by Pancho Villa during the Battle of Ojinaga in 1918. As various factions competed for control of Mexico, the nation's bloody civil war raged on until General Álvaro Obregón assumed the presidency in 1920.

who were crossing the border every year to compete for jobs and housing with the lowest-paid and least-educated Americans.

Munguía brought his family 125 miles north of the Rio Grande to San Antonio, the scene of the most famous U.S.–Mexican conflict. In their new city, the Munguías settled in a neighborhood that was as Mexican as Mexico itself. Neither the climate, the architecture, the language, the customs, nor the cuisine betrayed the reality of the United States. But the apparent freedom of every person in San Antonio to voice any opinion, to campaign for any political candidate, to read or distribute to others any sort of printed matter, made it clear to the newcomers that they were now living in a democratic society.

Freedom of speech was especially important to a man like José Rómulo Munguía, who still earned his living in the printing trade. After working for a large Spanish-language newspaper in San Antonio for a few years, he set up his own business. Because of his hard work, the Munguías soon became one of the leading families in San Antonio's Mexican community. The Munguía children worked with their father after classes and on weekends, preparing to become full partners in the business after their graduation from high school.

Near the end of World War II in 1945, Elvira Munguía, one of José Rómulo's daughters, met George Cisneros, who had just returned from nearly three years of combat duty in the Pacific. He left the army as a high-ranking noncommissioned officer—a sergeant major—who had seen enough horrors in three years to last him many lifetimes. The two young people fell in love at first sight. Nevertheless, the customs of the times, as well as the traditions of Mexico, demanded a long and formal courtship. The couple's first date took place under the supervision of Elvira's brother, and her father's permission was an absolute requisite for their marriage.

George Cisneros was not Mexican but rather the descendant of early Spanish settlers who had colonized the American Southwest more than a century before the territory became part of the United States. His people had not come to the United States—the United States had come to them.

Cisneros was thus more of a "native American" than any but a handful of his fellow citizens. But because of his Spanish surname and dark skin, he was subjected to the same sorts of prejudice and bigotry as any Mexican immigrant who had just crossed the Rio Grande. Cisneros had grown used to this treatment, but his resentment and anger never left him. Nevertheless, he had his own way of dealing with racism: he determined to work harder, be stronger, and do better than those who ridiculed him.

Cisneros was so much like his father-in-law that the two men grew to have an enormous respect for each other. They had both seen the horrors of war, had both felt the sting of prejudice, had both known the deprivation of poverty. Both men had narrowly escaped death on more than one occasion, and both treasured the freedoms and opportunities America offered. Most important, they each loved Elvira wholeheartedly.

George Cisneros and Elvira Munguía were married in 1945, and two years later, their first child—

José Rómulo Munguía, the grandfather of Henry Cisneros, emigrated from Mexico to the United States in 1926. After surviving revolutions and death sentences, the outspoken journalist was eager to provide a safe and democratic environment for his children.

Henry Gabriel—was born. The child would be raised in a family that valued education above all else, and he would come to love the grandfather who taught him about the land on the other side of the Rio Grande. Even before he could read or write, Henry Cisneros would understand the vast differences between Mexico and the United States.

As Henry matured, his grandfather taught him the history of the Mexican people, and the elder man did not hide the personal sacrifices he had made or the hardships he had endured in an attempt to change that

George Cisneros, Sr., Henry's father, photographed in 1945. Cisneros, who saw action in the Pacific as a U.S. Army sergeant, was one of many Mexican Americans on the front lines during World War II (1941–45). During the war, Mexican Americans won more Congressional Medals of Honor than did any other ethnic group.

history. Henry understood from his earliest childhood that he was an American first but also a Mexican. He would come to be proud of both heritages, but his loyalties and allegiances were never confused. Henry's patriotic feelings toward America were only strengthened by hearing his grandfather's tales of oppression in Mexico.

José Rómulo Munguía, on the other hand, remained a Mexican citizen to the end. Although he lived in the United States for almost half a century, until his death in 1975, he refused to apply for American citizenship. For Munguía, Mexican citizenship was precious, despite his dislike of the various governments that had ruled the country of his birth.

Thanks to his parents' hard work, Henry's childhood was much more comfortable than theirs had been. George Cisneros had grown up on a hardscrabble farm in Colorado, in a family of 12 hungry children. Elvira Cisneros had come to the United States as an impoverished little girl whose father was trying to stay one step ahead of the firing squad. But George and Elvira's children never knew hard times. They lived in a section of San Antonio known as Prospect Hill, only a short walk from the worst Mexican slums of San Antonio's inner city but a whole world away from the deprivations endured by most of the city's Mexican population.

It would have been easy enough for Henry and his brothers and sisters to forget their heritage and melt into the fabric of American suburbia the way so many other children and grandchildren of immigrants did in the great cultural assimilation that followed World War II. The millions of young sailors and soldiers who had survived the ravages of the war returned home with an entirely new perspective. They were impatient, and in many cases, intolerant. They understandably wanted to take their families away from the

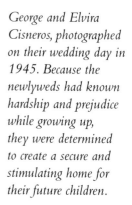

George and Elvira Cisneros, photographed on their wedding day in 1945. Because the newlyweds had known hardship and prejudice while growing up, they were determined to create a secure and stimulating home for their future children.

problems of the cities, but they also wanted to take their families away from other racial and ethnic groups whom they found objectionable.

It is odd to think that discrimination could actually contribute to the viability of an ethnic community, but it is true. Those ethnic groups of European extraction—the Irish, Italians, Poles, Jews, and Germans—were readily accepted as part of mainstream America's new suburbia. After the war ended, millions of so-called tract houses were built. Each development consisted of hundreds or even thousands of nearly identical homes, and the homes were sold to people with nearly identical values. The suburbs were popu-

lated almost entirely by Americans of European ancestry. Because of this mass exodus to the suburbs, most
lighter-skinned ethnic groups lost both their cultural
identity and the political clout they had enjoyed in the
cities, where their concentrated voting power had
influenced the workings of government.

Mexican Americans, on the other hand, were not
easily assimilated into this new suburban society. They
were usually darker skinned, normally did not speak
English as a first language, and often did not speak
English at all. As a result, they were viewed both as
"foreigners" and as a distinct, nonwhite, racial entity—
although Mexico's heritage is primarily a combina-
tion of European, North American Indian, and Asian
influences. Because Mexican Americans were per-
ceived this way by other Americans, and because they
typically were able to find work only in the lowest-
paid occupations, their culture was not diluted or
destroyed by the "homogenizing" of America.

The Mexican Americans in San Antonio and
other southwestern cities grew stronger because they
were forced to remain together. As Earl Shorris points
out in his book *Latinos: A Biography of the People,* the
wartime exploits of Mexican Americans such as
George Cisneros left them with a new sense of pride
and urgency: "A people that had won more Medals of
Honor than any other racial or ethnic group during
the war could not feel quite so humble at home. . . .
Men who had commanded Anglo troops in battle did
not cringe before them in civilian life. . . . Sergeants
and captains and buck privates turned into professional men and entrepreneurs; the vets no longer felt
like intruders in a strange country." The political
awakening of Mexican Americans—still decades away
from fulfillment—was virtually assured by the complex set of circumstances that kept them isolated in
their own urban communities.

A CULTURE
PRESERVED

Henry and Pauline Cisneros pose on the front lawn of the family's comfortable home in San Antonio, at the beginning of the 1950s. Though Mexican Americans often faced harsh discrimination in the Southwest, San Antonians such as George Cisneros were able to find good jobs at local U.S. Defense Department facilities.

enry Cisneros's neighborhood, Prospect Hill, had once been filled by German immigrants and their descendants, but it was gradually transformed by a middle-class and upwardly mobile Mexican-American influx. The transformation of Prospect Hill represented, in some ways, a model of how the state of Texas itself had been transformed throughout its long and unpredictable history.

Prospect Hill was also a "military" neighborhood, whose residents were employed primarily by the United States government at several nearby defense installations. Earl Shorris has explained the role of the federal government in creating a Mexican-American middle class in Prospect Hill:

San Antonio, Texas, indicates what might have happened had racism not prevented Latinos from following the European model earlier on. The Department of Defense, which had been the largest employer in the area for many years, established equitable policies for civilian employees long before many states and municipalities. Although Latinos were prevented from taking full advantage of the federal policies by the blatantly discriminatory policies of the local school system, which did not prepare them as well as Anglos for civil service examinations,

they were able to find work on the nearby army
and air force bases at fair wages.

Some Prospect Hill residents were on active duty with
the armed services while others were civilian employees. Because of this dependence on government employment, the neighborhood as a whole tended to be
conventional, conservative, and promilitary. George
Cisneros, for example, remained active in the U.S.
Army Reserve, and he eventually achieved the rank of
lieutenant colonel. During the 1960s, when the Vietnam War developed into a major conflict, the army
recalled him to active duty. There was no resentment
on George Cisneros's part when he received his or-
ders, though. An extraordinarily patriotic man, he was
proud to serve his country at any age. Henry Cisneros
recently recalled, "My father had General Douglas
MacArthur's farewell address taped up at home—
right on his closet door. It was a wonderful speech,
one of the best I've ever read."

At that time, Henry was a senior in high school.
George Cisneros remained on active duty for the next
three years at Fort Sam Houston; fortunately, he was
not sent back into combat in Vietnam. Still, the situation created stress for the Cisneros family. During the
entire three years, George Cisneros could have been
sent overseas at any time; other senior officers he
knew were sent to Vietnam, and some were killed in
action.

Throughout most of Henry's boyhood, the Cisneroses were in many ways a typical American family
in the 1950s mode. His father worked hard outside the
home, while his mother raised the children and
worked just as hard or even harder in the home.
George and Elvira Cisneros attended church on Sun-
days, socialized with their neighbors on weekends, and
were extremely involved in their children's lives, particularly their education.

In other ways, however, the Cisneroses were distinctly different from most Americans. They were bilingual; Henry learned to speak Spanish fluently before he learned English. (By the time he was in high school, however, English was spoken more often than Spanish inside the Cisneros home.) The Cisneroses belonged to a community with distinct social customs that had been founded upon centuries of experience in Mexico. Most important, the Cisneroses' physical

Henry Cisneros poses in his Little League uniform during the late 1950s. Though he enjoyed a comfortable all-American boyhood, Henry was also taught by his grandfather to be proud of his Mexican heritage and to sympathize with the plight of the poor.

characteristics would never be mistaken for those of the average American—at least not in the 1950s. Blond hair, blue eyes, and pale skin were not prevalent in the Mexican community. Nevertheless, Henry Cisneros later declared that he did not recall any overt acts of discrimination as a child. "In San Antonio, Mexicans had a place in the system," he explained. "Our day-to-day lives were pretty normal, really. There were 16 boys about my age who lived on our block—so we spent a lot of time playing baseball and football. My community was like one of those Norman Rockwell paintings, except all of the faces were brown!"

While Henry was growing up, his grandfather continued to grow in stature in San Antonio's Mexican community. He was exceptionally well read and maintained a vast personal library, much of it dedicated to Mexican history. In time, he became one of the community's elder statesmen, particularly as the

The Cisneros family—left to right: Pauline, Elvira, Tina, George, Jr., George, Sr., Henry, and Tim— pose for a portrait in 1965. At the time of the photo, George, Sr., was an officer in the U.S. Army Reserve, and Henry was a cadet in his high school's ROTC program.

second, and third, and even fourth generations of Mexican Americans were born in San Antonio.

Henry had two brothers—George, Jr., and Tim—and two sisters—Tina and Pauline. The five children formed an intellectual group, and not by accident. George and Elvira Cisneros saw to it that their children's lives were carefully structured and orchestrated to achieve certain goals. Reading and conversation were of particular importance in the Cisneros household—these were daily activities that became deeply ingrained in Henry's personality at an early age. But the Cisneroses did not simply want their children to learn; they wanted them to ask questions as well. Strong disagreement and vigorous debate were not vices in the Cisneros household—they were virtues.

All five children attended a private Catholic grammar school. Henry did so well in the classroom that he was allowed to skip a grade, making him a year or more younger than most of his classmates. This was no impediment to his performance, though, and he continued to place at or near the top of his class in most subjects. Cisneros often commented later on the value of a Catholic education, partly because it stressed more than academic achievement. He felt that the moral and social values he was taught as a child helped to instill integrity and compassion. Throughout his life, Cisneros was clearly a "winner" in the sense that he was always able to achieve his goals and reap the rewards. Unlike many people who fit that category, his deepest concerns were for those less fortunate. His youthful idealism did not fade with time but rather became better defined and more powerful during his years of public service.

During the 1960s, many high schools—particularly those in the South—had Reserve Officers' Training Corps (ROTC) programs, and San Antonio's Central Catholic High School was no exception. The

ROTC program, affiliated with the Department of Defense, prepared students for military careers after graduation. Henry became an ROTC cadet in high school, and he had hopes of being admitted to the United States Air Force Academy in Colorado Springs, Colorado. He almost made it, but he was younger than most other high school students when he applied, and reportedly this counted heavily against him. He was, after all, still a few weeks short of his 17th birthday when he graduated from high school, whereas many of his classmates were 18 or older.

As a member of the Corps of Cadets at Texas A & M University, Cisneros tackles one of the less glamorous aspects of military life. Though he began his college career as only an average student, he improved his grades dramatically during his junior and senior years.

Being turned down by the Air Force Academy may have saved Henry Cisneros's life. If he had been accepted, he would have graduated in the class of 1968 and almost certainly would have been sent to Vietnam, where almost 2 million air force personnel served; of these, 2,500 (mostly pilots and flight crew members) were killed in action. Instead, Cisneros enrolled at Texas A & M, a private university which, at that time, was also a military school. Every student at A & M was required to join the school's Corps of Cadets, and Cisneros was happy to do so. He enjoyed the military regimen and the precision and discipline it brought to his life.

Cisneros excelled at Texas A & M, holding a number of important offices in various student organizations. He was not really a top student, but his grades improved noticeably in his final two years. Cisneros had tremendous energy, so much so that he usually took on more responsibility and engaged in more diverse activities than any human being could successfully accommodate. But this quality would serve Cisneros well in later years, and his confidence in the face of challenge would enable him to become an American political legend before he reached his 35th birthday.

THE PUBLIC GOOD

While Cisneros was studying at Texas A & M, the United States—under the leadership of President Lyndon B. Johnson—was becoming increasingly enmeshed in what would become one of this country's greatest political and military misadventures. The American involvement in the Southeast Asian nation of Vietnam began in the 1950s, when President Dwight D. Eisenhower sent "advisers" to South Vietnam to aid the government in its fight against an insurgent army of guerrilla fighters known as the Vietcong. The role of the advisers changed in the early 1960s, as they increased in number and accompanied Vietnamese forces on military excursions. Before long, U.S. troops were engaged directly in a full-scale war against both the Vietcong and the armed forces of Communist-led North Vietnam.

Popular sentiment against U.S. military actions in Vietnam gained steam in 1964, and the protest rapidly grew in strength so that by the late 1960s or early 1970s it included the majority of American voters. Meanwhile, a disproportionate number of black and Latino soldiers were dying in the fields, jungles, and rice paddies of Vietnam. Even though Cisneros was a cadet at a military college and his father was a high-ranking army officer, it was impossible for him not to question the morality of the war in Vietnam.

The war in Vietnam was a particularly bloody conflict. The weekly total of U.S. soldiers killed in

Wearing the full-dress uniform of a Texas A & M cadet, Cisneros poses for his college graduation photo. As a student, Cisneros had sometimes tried to do too many things at once; after graduation, his enormous energy enabled him to hold a full-time job while also continuing his education.

55

action sometimes rose to over 500—more than the total number of American troops who were killed in the Persian Gulf war of 1990–91. By the end of the conflict, 58,000 Americans would lose their lives.

When Cisneros graduated from Texas A & M in June 1968, the war was at its height, and the divisions in American society between the "hawks" who supported the war and the "doves" who opposed it were ugly indeed. The college campuses of the nation had become bastions of antiwar sentiment and the breeding grounds of political actions that sometimes went beyond marches and demonstrations. Rioting, arson, bombings, and sabotage were occasionally employed by the most radical opponents of the war, who believed that their actions were justified because they would hasten the end of the war and save the lives of Vietnamese civilians. Indeed, many hundreds of thousands of entirely innocent Vietnamese had been killed or wounded in the fighting.

Marchers protesting U.S. involvement in Vietnam picket the White House in March 1966. Though Cisneros came from a highly patriotic family and served in the National Guard, he was disturbed by the terrible human cost of the war in Southeast Asia.

On the whole, 1968 was a year of great turmoil in the United States. Two American leaders who spoke passionately about the need for change—the Reverend Martin Luther King, Jr., and Senator Robert F. Kennedy—were assassinated. King, the acknowledged leader of the civil rights movement, was shot dead by a sniper in Memphis, Tennessee, on April 4. His death touched off a wave of destructive riots in a number of U.S. cities, as African Americans reacted with anger and despair to the slaying of the man who had spearheaded their drive for social justice.

Kennedy, who seemed certain to win the Democratic presidential nomination, was murdered just two months later as he celebrated his victory in California's June 5 primary election. As Kennedy delivered his victory speech to an elated crowd of supporters in a Los Angeles hotel, an assassin waited in the hallway. When Kennedy left the hotel ballroom, he was shot at close range with a handgun. His supporters had believed that Kennedy, if elected president, would quickly end the war in Vietnam and unite the nation behind a program of social reform; with his death, those hopes were dashed.

The assassinations of 1968 forever changed the lives of those who were working for peace and civil rights in America. King and Kennedy joined a long list of men and women who, collectively, represented America's blood sacrifice for justice. Against the backdrop of Vietnam—which each week sent planeload after planeload of flag-draped coffins home for military funerals—the nation's young idealists seemed much older when 1968 came to an end. Henry Cisneros was one of them; he had been profoundly affected by the martyrdom of the two great leaders.

The war in Vietnam effectively ended the political career of President Lyndon B. Johnson. After nearly losing the New Hampshire Democratic primary elec-

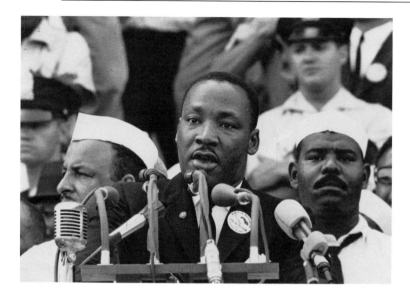

The Reverend Martin Luther King, Jr., leader of the civil rights movement in the United States, delivers his classic "I Have a Dream" speech in 1963. After King was gunned down by a sniper in April 1968, riots erupted in many U.S. cities. Only two months apart, the assassinations of King and Robert F. Kennedy were among the most shattering events in U.S. history.

tion to Senator Eugene McCarthy of Minnesota, Johnson became the first U.S. president since Calvin Coolidge in the 1920s to decide not to run for reelection. Though his commitment to the war in Vietnam cost him the White House, Johnson did have strong support for his domestic policies. After he signed the Civil Rights of Act of 1964 into law, Johnson embarked on a progressive—and expensive—social policy that he called the War on Poverty. Under the Johnson administration (1964–68), the federal government created a whole new crop of social programs providing housing, food, medical care, education, job training, and child care. U.S. taxpayers financed both of Johnson's wars, and some historians would eventually come to regard even the well-intentioned War on Poverty as an expensive failure. But in 1966, when Johnson created the Model Cities program, he was still firmly in power, and he ruled the Congress with an iron hand.

The Model Cities program designated more than 100 cities across the nation as being worthy of federal aid for urban renewal. Like many of Johnson's programs, it had a catchy name that evoked an image of a newer, brighter, refurbished America. But, also like most of Johnson's programs, it was just another vehicle for the president's "pork barrel" politics—a way for Johnson to pay off political debts to his friends and divert federal funds into areas that were most vital to his reelection campaign.

On the local level, however, some of the nation's most idealistic, dedicated, and self-sacrificing young leaders were to be found working long hours in rough neighborhoods for paupers' wages. Henry Cisneros was one of them. The politicians in Washington might just be playing games, but Cisneros and those who worked with him were deadly serious about using the funds available to them to make substantial and permanent improvements to the quality of life in their communities. In January 1969, six months after he went to work for the Model Cities program in San Antonio, Cisneros was named assistant director. He was only 21 years old.

Cisneros became an effective intermediary between San Antonio's large, poor Mexican underclass and the mostly white, English-speaking public officials at city hall. As the Model Cities program began to make real improvements to the quality of daily life in the community, it grew in strength and influence. San Antonio's Mexicans were, at the same time, organizing politically and becoming a powerful force for change in local government. Years later, Cisneros stated that he had learned everything he knew about the mechanics of making government work for the good of the people during his years with the Model Cities program. This hands-on training in government was not the only benefit; Cisneros also made political contacts with hundreds of people and performed favors or services for thousands more. In that short period of time in his early twenties, Cisneros established the core of a political machine that would assure his success in local elections for the next two decades.

However, politics was not the only thing in Cisneros's life. When he was only 14 years old, he had met a girl named Mary Alice Pérez at a neighborhood baseball game. Pérez was two years younger than Cisneros, so he had no thought of dating her at the time. But the two young people continued to see one another at various social functions of San Antonio's Mexican-American community. They liked one another, though their relationship could not be described as a case of love at first sight. In fact, Mary Alice thought that Cisneros was rather ugly: he was tall and skinny and had big ears. She also found him arrogant. More than two years would pass before Cisneros and Pérez began dating, and even then, their courtship would be carried out under the strict control that was still exercised by Mexican-American families.

The couple's first actual date took place in 1963, the year when the United States Supreme Court ruled that mandatory prayer in the public schools was

Robert F. Kennedy makes a campaign stop in Long Beach, New York, during his successful run for the U.S. Senate in 1964. Kennedy's 1968 assassination was a painful blow to young idealists such as Cisneros; they believed that if Kennedy had become president, he could have united the nation behind a program of social reform.

unconstitutional, and the year that President John F. Kennedy was assassinated in Dallas, Texas. There were great changes taking place in the everyday lives of Americans—changes in values, religion, politics, and personal behavior. These changes were affecting the Mexican-American community of San Antonio as well, although in 1963, relations between the sexes were still often governed by rules that may appear to be old-fashioned by the standards of the 1990s. Long engagements were quite common, and it was not considered unusual in 1963 for a couple to date for weeks or even months before exchanging their first kiss.

Cisneros and Pérez continued to date for six years. While Cisneros attended Texas A & M, Pérez remained in San Antonio, working during the day and taking college courses at night. After receiving his bachelor's degree in liberal arts from Texas A & M, Cisneros continued his studies there, earning a master's degree in urban and regional planning just one year later. Finally, in June 1969, after Cisneros had established himself as assistant director in the Model Cities program, he and Pérez were ready to marry.

In 1970, the newlyweds moved to Washington, D.C., the first home for either of them outside Texas. Cisneros had been accepted into George Washington University's Ph.D. program, where he would continue his studies in urban planning and public administration. The Cisneroses had very little money; his Model Cities program job and her clerical positions had barely enabled them to make ends meet in San Antonio, let alone put aside any savings. Nevertheless, they were young and hopeful and willing to take risks. In fact, when they arrived in Washington, the Cisneroses had neither a place to live nor any prospect of steady employment.

Before long, though, Mary Alice found a job at a local bank. Henry went to work for the National

League of Cities, a private organization that acts as an advocate for 1,500 of the city governments in the United States. Financed by dues from its member cities, and with a staff of 75, the league has helped bridge the gap between cities and the federal government since 1924. Even with their combined salaries, the Cisneroses did not earn much, but they somehow managed to pay the rent on their small apartment and keep food on the table.

At work, Cisneros learned everything he could about the practical aspects of urban management. At night, he studied theories of city government in his courses at George Washington University. His combined work and study schedule was grueling, sometimes exceeding 100 hours per week, but he knew that he was preparing for the kind of career he really wanted. As his thinking grew more focused, he had a revelation about his ambitions: "I knew for a long time that I wanted to be in public service and in urban service," he recalled. "But I eventually realized that some changes had to come politically—they had to be fostered at a higher level."

Henry could not spend as much time at home as either he or Mary Alice would have liked, but they were willing to make the necessary sacrifices for the good of his future career. Nevertheless, life in Washington was not easy for Mary Alice, more than 1,500 miles away from her family in San Antonio, with a husband who was often away from home. In addition to his time in the office and the classroom, Cisneros was often forced to travel on National League of Cities business. When the Cisneroses' first child, Teresa, was born a couple of weeks prematurely in 1971, Henry was in Florida. Throughout his professional life, he was repeatedly confronted with the conflict between his family responsibilities and his public duties.

Shortly after their 1969 wedding, pictured here, Henry and Mary Alice Cisneros moved to Washington, D.C., so that Henry could begin his career in public service and attend graduate school. Life was not easy for the young Texans, but their efforts were rewarded in 1971 when Henry was named a White House Fellow.

Around the time of his daughter's birth, Cisneros applied for a position in the White House Fellows program, which each year accepted about two dozen young scholars to work with senior officials of the president's administration. Lyndon Johnson had introduced the program during his tenure in office, and it had been continued by President Richard M. Nixon, who had been elected in 1968. The White House Fellows program was very competitive—each year thousands of outstanding applicants vied for the handful of open places.

Cisneros was one of the few to be accepted. He began working with Elliot Richardson, the secretary of health, education, and welfare. Richardson, an elegant, Harvard-educated New Englander, became as much of a mentor and friend to Cisneros as he was an employer. Richardson sincerely liked Cisneros on a personal level, and he frequently invited Henry and Mary Alice to social functions at the White House. He gave his young protégé some advice, too, as Cisneros recently recalled. "He told me that working hard and doing a good job would ultimately lead to success, much more so than trying to plan out a political career. I took that advice, and he was right."

CISNEROS
THE CANDIDATE

Cisneros takes part in a community protest march in San Antonio during the early 1970s. Though Cisneros returned to his native city in 1974 as a professor at the University of Texas, he was soon caught up in the political ferment sweeping San Antonio's Mexican-American neighborhoods.

During his year as a White House Fellow, Henry Cisneros continued his doctoral studies at George Washington University. After earning his Ph.D. in public administration in 1971, he began to serve a two-year military commitment. By this time, the war in Vietnam was winding down rapidly, and the armed forces were not sending large numbers of fresh troops to Southeast Asia. As a result, Cisneros was able to fulfill his obligations by serving in the Massachusetts National Guard. As a member of the guard, he had to spend several weeks a year in training at Fort Benning, Georgia, but he was otherwise free to pursue his professional career. After his ROTC training at Texas A & M, Cisneros adapted readily to the military routine. When he left the National Guard in 1973, he had achieved the rank of captain, having been promoted twice during his brief period of service.

After Cisneros's year as a White House Fellow ended in 1972, he and his family headed for Boston, where he began work on a second master's degree, in public administration, at Harvard University's prestigious John F. Kennedy School of Government. He earned the degree in one year and took a job as a teaching assistant at the Massachusetts Institute of Technology, where he also began work on a second doctoral degree. Still just 26 years old, Cisneros already possessed a bachelor's degree, two master's degrees, and a doctorate—and he was still seeking more education.

In 1974, the Cisneroses decided to return to their home city of San Antonio. Henry knew that it was time to begin to put all of his classroom learning into action, and Mary Alice wanted to go home to Texas to raise her children among friends and family in a familiar environment. She had no idea that within a year Cisneros would be nationally famous and that the entire Cisneros family would become the subject of great attention from the local and national media.

Through custom rather than by law, San Antonio had developed an unusual political tradition, one that differed markedly from the system governing national elections in the United States. Rather than making the usual choice between Democrats, Republicans, and members of other parties, voters in San Antonio chose their elected officials from among a field of independent candidates, some of whom were affiliated with various local civic organizations. Although some candidates were known to belong to one party or another, other candidates were either entirely unaffiliated or only loosely connected with one of the major parties. Because of this custom, the usual distinctions between political parties, and the sharp ideological differences between conservatives and liberals, became somewhat blurred. One positive aspect of San Antonio's elective process, however, was that the voters were given the opportunity to select from among a field of well-qualified candidates without feeling that they were deserting the party they usually voted for.

One of San Antonio's strongest political organizations had, none too modestly, named itself the Good Government League. Known locally as the GGL, the league had virtually controlled the city's government since the late 1950s. The GGL was dominated by white, middle-class civic leaders and local merchants; its political orientation was conservative and pro-business. But there were also substantial reform elements to be found within the organization, and these forces were astute enough, by the early 1970s, to realize that the GGL would not survive for much longer unless it expanded its ranks and embraced the culture and political aspirations of the city's growing Mexican community.

When the Cisneroses returned to San Antonio in 1974, Henry joined the faculty at the University of Texas as an assistant professor. But within weeks of his return to his native city, Cisneros—along with many

A view of San Antonio, which became one of the 10 largest cities in the United States during the 1970s. San Antonio's unusual voting system, in which all candidates ran as independents, made it possible for newcomers such as Cisneros to have an impact on the city's political life.

other Mexican Americans—found himself engulfed by the tidal wave of political activity that was sweeping through San Antonio's Mexican neighborhoods. After more than a century of quiet obedience to the city's ruling class, San Antonio's Mexican Americans were determined to attain their fair share of political power. They wanted a voice in how their city was run, and they wanted a say in their children's and grandchildren's future.

José Rómulo Munguía, Cisneros's grandfather, who had arrived in San Antonio almost 50 years before, was thrilled by the idea that San Antonio's Mexicans could finally achieve—through the democratic process—the sort of political influence that had been denied to them in Mexico. His joy at this prospect was even greater when he saw his own grandson being courted by many of the city's political leaders, from both the Mexican and Anglo communities.

Progressive members of the Good Government League were by this time desperately searching for Mexican candidates whose educational and professional credentials were equal to or better than those of the non-Mexican candidates, and whose family backgrounds and political ideas would not seem threatening to San Antonio's white middle-class voters. Cisneros came as close to this description as anyone they could find. As a former employee of a conservative Republican president, the son of a career officer in the U.S. Army, and an energetic but soft-spoken young man with an Ivy League education, he seemed to be the answer to all their prayers. His family's patriotism and stability, his strong San Antonio roots, and his obvious concern for the city's future would certainly make him acceptable to even the most cautious and conservative voters.

In addition to all his other assets, Cisneros already had a huge political base in San Antonio. A politician's base is like a football team's home field. It does not guarantee victory, but it greatly improves one's chances. Cisneros's grandfather's connections alone assured massive grass-roots support in the city's Mexican community. In addition, Cisneros's years of service with the Model Cities program had earned him thousands of supporters in San Antonio, including many hundreds in the Anglo community.

Still, Cisneros had to fight hard to get on the ballot in early 1975. Several of his family members had strongly suggested to the leaders of the Good Government League that Cisneros would be an ideal candidate for the San Antonio City Council. The GGL was not easily convinced, though. Some thought Cisneros's politics were too liberal for San Antonio's voters, and Cisneros was only 27 years old—just a kid, some of them thought when they interviewed him one winter night. Still, the most important thing to the GGL's leaders was to elect as many candidates as possible, and Cisneros certainly looked like a winner.

Speaking of elections, Cisneros later said that winning is "a reflection on one's abilities." By the same token, so is losing. Cisneros is thus not inclined to make excuses for a setback or to claim that his victories have been a matter of luck. His view is that of a man who hates the idea of defeat and invests a great amount of personal pride in his chosen ventures, no matter how great the odds against him. During his first political campaign, Cisneros—like his rebel grandfather who looked death in the face more than once—demonstrated a steely determination to prevail. His quiet, polite, self-effacing manner was not insincere by any means, but anyone who mistook his low-key manner for weakness quickly learned the error of that judgment.

With the Good Government League's endorsement, Cisneros began his campaign. San Antonio had

never seen anything quite like it. The Cisneros family—including aunts, uncles, cousins, siblings, nieces,
nephews, parents, and grandparents—joined with
other Cisneros supporters to unleash one of the most
enthusiastic and energetic campaigns in the city's history. At the heart of the campaign was the Cisneros
family print shop, which proved invaluable to the
effort. It churned out hundreds of thousands of pieces
of campaign literature, in English and Spanish, which
the volunteers distributed by hand throughout the
entire city. Cisneros's bid for office was not a "Mexican" effort, per se; he campaigned just as hard in the
white neighborhoods of San Antonio as he did in the
middle-class Mexican areas and the inner-city barrios.

Cisneros proved his independence early in the
campaign. He broke with a tradition that dictated

*Shortly after his election
to San Antonio's City
Council, Cisneros asks
students about their
concerns during a visit to
the Riley School. As the
holder of a bachelor's degree,
two master's degrees, and
two doctorates, Cisneros was
well qualified to discuss
the value of education.*

low-key, relaxed, "gentlemanly" campaigning by the candidates. Cisneros had a problem with that kind of campaigning: he did not want to be remembered as a gentleman; he wanted to win. In order for his victory to be assured, Cisneros knew that he would have to campaign aggressively, 16 to 18 hours a day, 7 days a week. If the other GGL candidates could not keep up with him, that was their problem. If they did not hunger for victory as much as he did, they might lose in their bids for office, but he would not lose his. That was the attitude shared by Cisneros and his entire campaign organization. Victory was nonnegotiable for Cisneros, and throughout his long political career that stance would never be changed or modified.

In April 1975, Henry Gabriel Cisneros, still two months shy of his 28th birthday, became the youngest person ever elected to the San Antonio City Council. Prophetically, he did even better in the white neighborhoods than in those voting districts that were primarily Mexican. In the Mexican districts, he was actually hurt by his endorsement from the conservative Good Government League, which was so closely identified with the city's Anglo power structure. Nevertheless, anyone who wanted to go far in San Antonio politics would have to be able to appeal to white voters, and Cisneros had proved in his very first bid for office that he could meet that test.

A DELICATE
BALANCE

Councilman Cisneros takes part in a touch football game as part of a campaign to bring a professional football franchise to San Antonio. During his tenure on the city council, Cisneros was tireless in his efforts to help San Antonio attract new businesses and investments.

Nineteen seventy-five was a year filled with both triumph and sadness for the Cisneros family. A month after the elections, Henry and Mary Alice had another event to celebrate, the birth of their second daughter, Mercedes Cristina. At the end of the year, however, the family suffered a great loss when José Rómulo Munguía, the valiant revolutionary and family patriarch, died at the age of 93.

Henry Cisneros had fulfilled his grandfather's dream, and now he had to go the rest of the way on his own. After carefully reviewing the election results from San Antonio's many voting districts, Cisneros knew beyond a doubt that his political future would lie not in the hands of his Mexican-American supporters but rather in his appeal to a broad cross section of voters. In fact, Cisneros did about twice as well as any other GGL candidate in the Mexican neighborhoods, but would have done far better without the GGL's endorsement. On the other hand, without the GGL's backing, he would not have been able to get enough non-Mexican support to win the election at all.

Cisneros's first act as an elected official was to declare his independence to the voters of San Antonio. He made it clear that the GGL's endorsement did not obligate him in any way and that he would be as willing to confront the GGL as any other political organization in San Antonio.

Cisneros faced many challenges in his new job. The election of one or two Mexican Americans to the San Antonio City Council did little to calm the growing racial tensions in the city; if anything, success at the polls may have emboldened the more radical elements in the Mexican community, which had many legitimate grievances. In the early 1970s, Mexican Americans were reaching a point in their own civil rights movement similar to that reached by African Americans a decade before. Mexican Americans experienced widespread discrimination in employment and housing, and they had the additional difficulty of the long-standing language barrier that often separated them from the greater society.

Cisneros personally supported the Mexican-American civil rights movement. Even though he had grown up in a secure middle-class neighborhood, he had always cared deeply about the deprivations of San Antonio's poorest Mexicans. José Rómulo Munguía's influence had assured that Cisneros would never forget his roots. But Cisneros also believed that the tactics of the more radical Mexican-American activists would accomplish nothing positive and might even scare away businesses from San Antonio, thus hindering the city's economic development. This would result in fewer jobs, more unemployment, and more poverty. As a realist, Cisneros knew that without a strong business climate, all San Antonio's people would suffer. Gradually, Cisneros began to develop a reputation as a centrist, or moderate. Some Mexican Americans accused him of "selling out," or becoming too conservative, but he would not back down.

Cisneros argued that he represented all of San Antonio's citizens, not just those of Mexican heritage. He also knew that the best way to serve his own people would be to build bridges between them and San Antonio's non-Mexican residents and with business interests from outside the state.

In 1975, San Antonio—if considered at all—was thought of by many Americans as just a sleepy little town in Texas. It was, in fact, the nation's 10th-largest city, and Cisneros knew that a change of image would help to attract new businesses to the area. One of his highest priorities as a council member was to encourage new investment in San Antonio. He often traveled far from home to meet with business people in their corporate boardrooms and "pitch" San Antonio to them. Most other council members lacked the confidence and sophistication to attempt such initiatives, but this was never a problem with Cisneros. His experience in Washington, particularly his year as a White House Fellow, had helped him develop the poise, persuasiveness, and diplomatic skills that were needed to lure some of the country's leading businesses to San Antonio.

Eventually, some Mexican-American groups accused Cisneros of betraying their cause, but it is doubtful that these groups actually represented any more than a small minority of San Antonio's Latino voters. Cisneros found it hard to take when some of his own people criticized him more severely than any of the non-Mexican groups, but he was never known to be swayed by pressure tactics. Though he was criticized by opponents as being too dry and practical—one critic said that he had a "cut and paste mind"—Cisneros recognized the dangers of political proposals that were based on emotional considerations rather than logic.

As a council member, Cisneros focused on issues that could unite the city's diverse ethnic groups. In particular, he challenged the large utility companies that had provided services to the city for decades. No

voter, whether white, black, or Latino, wanted to pay excessive fees for essential items such as telephone service, heat, or water, and the cost of these utilities was rising dramatically in the 1970s. Cisneros had the courage to take on the utilities and the wise political instincts to realize that he could broaden his political base by doing so.

One of Cisneros's first battles was fought with Southwestern Bell when the company tried to raise telephone rates for residential customers in San Antonio. Cisneros did not just oppose the increases; that would have been too simple and not dramatic enough to warrant press coverage. Instead, Cisneros challenged

Making the rounds with one of San Antonio's sanitation crews, Cisneros gets a nuts-and-bolts view of the city's services. His willingness to get his hands dirty made Councilman Henry, as he soon became known, a popular figure with both the voters and the Texas news media.

the company's entire rating structure, claiming that customers in the city's older neighborhoods (which were predominantly Mexican) were being forced to subsidize the wiring of phone lines for newly constructed, mostly Anglo neighborhoods. Cisneros stated that if people could afford expensive new homes, then they could afford to pay for their own telephone wiring. When the issue was presented in these terms, Southwestern Bell was forced to modify its policies.

Cisneros also challenged the leading local supplier of natural gas, which had breached its contract with the city of San Antonio by jacking up its prices during an energy crisis. Once again, Cisneros had chosen a target that almost every voter could hate. Even so, many of the city's wealthier residents were mistrustful of Cisneros. As time went on, even they were forced to admit that he was not at all interested in stirring up racial conflict. If anything, Cisneros's one true constituency comprised the lower economic and social classes, regardless of race or ethnicity. He also went out of his way to take an interest in the problems of San Antonio's municipal workers; at one point, he even rode the city's garbage trucks so that he could get a firsthand view of the everyday challenges faced by the sanitation crews. The news media loved it and soon referred to Cisneros simply as Councilman Henry, fostering the image of a sympathetic, down-to-earth official who cared about ordinary people.

When Cisneros was first elected to office, Lila Cockrell was the mayor of San Antonio. Although she came from the city's establishment, Cockrell was basically a moderate, and the fact that the voters of San Antonio were liberal enough to elect a woman mayor during the mid-1970s demonstrates the city's unusual political climate. Cisneros had an interesting relationship with Mayor Cockrell. Although they often locked horns over various issues, the two politicians shared a mutual respect. From time to time, they even helped one another during election campaigns.

Shortly after Cisneros was elected to the city council, the U.S. Department of Justice completed a long investigation of San Antonio's governmental practices. The Justice Department claimed that the city's method of electing council members violated federal law, in that it denied a fair chance of representation to the city's minorities. All of San Antonio's council members were elected "at large," which meant that every voter in the city considered each candidate. The Justice Department held that the council members should be elected by voting district, so that black and Mexican voters in San Antonio could be represented in a way that was roughly proportionate to their population in the city.

The city council was faced with a dilemma. Should it accept the federal order, or should it wage a long, expensive, and racially divisive battle in the federal courts, a battle it would probably lose? Mayor Cockrell and several other moderates joined Cisneros and other Mexican Americans on the council in voting to comply with the federal order. In 1976, the council changed the city charter to comply with the federal voting regulations. No one realized it at the time, but the change paved the way for Cisneros to become the city's mayor five years later.

The new city charter called for each of San Antonio's 11 council members to be elected by district, starting with the 1977 elections. Mayor Cockrell, who was seeking reelection, would still be drawing votes from the city as a whole, but she was certainly in trouble. San Antonio's conservatives were angry at her for not fighting the federal redistricting plan, and she was also facing a challenge from José San Martín, a Mexican American who had requested Cisneros's endorsement. Wisely, Cisneros remained "neutral" in the

Lila Cockrell served as mayor of San Antonio from 1975 to 1981. During Cisneros's tenure on the city council, he and Cockrell often clashed on matters of policy; however, they shared a mutual respect and actually helped one another during political campaigns.

mayoral race. For Cockrell, however, Cisneros's failure to come out for San Martín was very close to being an endorsement of her own candidacy.

The 1977 elections forever changed San Antonio's political landscape. Mayor Cockrell was reelected, but 6 of the 11 city council seats were now held by minorities—five Mexican Americans and one black candidate were successful in their bids for office. Cisneros himself faced no real opposition—he was reelected in a landslide, capturing more than 90 percent of the vote in his home district.

Cisneros's second term in office proved more difficult than his first. Only 30 years old when his new term began, Cisneros was still a bit naive about the ways of politics. Though some of his critics claimed that he was overly intellectual, he had a hot temper and a tendency toward impulsive behavior. At one point, he almost destroyed his political career entirely by making a play for power in the city council: he wanted to be officially recognized as the council's leader. On the surface, it appeared to Cisneros that he could not lose. He felt certain that he would have the

Cisneros emerges from a meeting at San Antonio's City Hall in 1978. Defeated in his 1977 bid to become the leader of the city council, Cisneros thought of resigning his post. However, his friends and relatives urged him to stay on, thus paving the way for his mayoral bid in 1981.

support of most, if not all, of the minority council
members, with the added backing of one or two
white moderates. In addition, he fully expected Mayor
Cockrell to endorse him, as a payback for his "neutrality" during the mayoral campaign.

Cisneros's youth and relative inexperience in office proved to be greater handicaps than he had realized. The other council members simply were not
ready to take direction from a 30-year-old with two
years' experience as a public official. In addition, some
of the other minority members had ambitions of their
own, and they feared giving Cisneros too much
power. He was defeated by one vote in his bid for the
city council leadership.

Cisneros was enraged by the defeat, and he threatened to resign from the city council. He even wrote
his resignation letter and distributed advance copies to
members of the local news media. Fortunately, older
and wiser members of the Cisneros political organization—particularly those of his parents' and grandparents' generations, whom he respected and trusted the
most—convinced him to remain in office. They knew
his time would come, and they were right.

Henry and Mary Alice Cisneros talk to reporters after Henry's overwhelming election as mayor of San Antonio in 1981. With his victory at the polls, Cisneros became the first American of Hispanic ancestry to be elected mayor of a major U.S. city.

CHAPTER

SEVEN

THE MAYOR'S OFFICE

In 1978, Henry Cisneros suffered another great political defeat when a $100 million bond proposal he supported was narrowly defeated by the voters of San Antonio. The bond package would have helped to revitalize some of the city's poorest neighborhoods, most of which were overwhelmingly Mexican. This time, however, Cisneros was more gracious in defeat. He kept his anger under control and remembered that he would have many opportunities in the future to make improvements in San Antonio's government.

The mayor and city council members served two-year terms in San Antonio, so political campaigning in the city was virtually a nonstop activity. Many of Cisneros's supporters urged him to run for mayor in 1979, which would have required him to challenge Mayor Cockrell, who had been in office for 4 years, after serving for 12 years as a member of the city council. Lila Cockrell was exceptionally popular in San Antonio, and Cisneros knew that it would be very tough to defeat her, especially because his own tenure in office had been only one-fourth as long as hers. Instead, he opted for the safe course, running for reelection to the city council. He was returned to office by another landslide.

By 1980, Cisneros had come to the conclusion that he would have to run for mayor of San Antonio in 1981, whether or not Cockrell sought reelection. His three terms on the city council had proven his

83

durability as a political candidate and had given him a
maturity that was likely to inspire much greater confidence from the city's voters. Moreover, his supporters
feared that if he remained on the city council, he
would become stagnant as a leader and as a candidate.
The natural rhythm of politics seemed to dictate that
1981 would be Cisneros's year to reach for the golden
ring, and by the autumn of 1980 he had made up his
mind. However, only his closest confidants and family
members knew that he was going to try for the
mayoralty.

Mayor Cockrell had been hinting to Cisneros for
months that she might not seek reelection. Her husband had suffered a heart attack, and she felt that the
strain of dealing with another campaign and another
two years of public life would be too much for him.
After 16 years of public service, Cockrell felt that she
was ready to leave office, but many of her advisers
were urging her to remain. It took her until December 1980 to make her decision; at that time, she
announced to the members of the press that she
would not seek another term as San Antonio's mayor.

Cisneros's supporters were elated. By the time of
Cockrell's announcement, Cisneros's campaign organization had been in place for months, with scores
of volunteers working around the clock. Cisneros's
brother George, who was serving as campaign man-
ager, ran the organization like a finely tuned military
regiment. Cisneros, who had been told in advance
of Mayor Cockrell's plans, announced his candidacy
immediately.

A number of prominent figures in San Antonio
were also interested in becoming mayor, including
several other Mexican Americans. Some of them were
considerably older than Cisneros, and they resented
the idea that someone so much younger would con-
sider himself fit to be San Antonio's mayor. From the

non-Mexican community, Cisneros's chief opponent was John Steen, who was also completing his third term on the city council.

Steen was a successful businessman who owned and operated several insurance agencies, and he had voted with Cisneros and Cockrell to comply with the federal order mandating single-district representation on the city council. As a moderate and a member of the business community, Steen possessed a large number of influential friends and supporters in San Antonio. On the negative side, Steen did not have the massive grass-roots campaign organization that the Cisneros family had been building for several decades. Steen had also lost the support of hard-line conservatives in San Antonio, who believed that he should have opposed the Justice Department redistricting order. Finally, Steen lacked the endorsement of Mayor Cockrell; she remained neutral during the campaign, but her neutrality was far more helpful to Cisneros than to Steen—it sent a signal to Anglo voters that there was nothing unacceptable or threatening about Cisneros.

On April 4, 1981, Henry Cisneros was elected mayor of San Antonio. With a population of 839,000, San Antonio was then the nation's ninth-largest city. Cisneros had become the first individual of Hispanic ancestry to be elected mayor of a city whose population ranked it as one of the nation's 10 largest. He was only 33 years old.

Numerically, Cisneros's victory was overwhelming—he received more than 60 percent of the vote. But Cisneros was not fooled by the numbers; he had realized long ago that simply winning an election would not change things for his people. He still had to convince the leaders of San Antonio's business community, as well as major American corporations, that the city would be a safe and profitable place to invest their money. Without an environment that was friendly to business, San Antonio would go the way of other decaying urban areas, Cisneros believed. This was perhaps the primary difference between Cisneros and other young, liberal politicians. Cisneros was an idealist, but only until he sat down and began negotiating—then he became a pragmatist who could bargain and compromise with the best of them.

When he took over as mayor, Cisneros also made it clear that he was prepared to directly attack social problems in the city. One of his first initiatives was a $60 million bond issue to revamp the city's drainage system. The issue was not a glamorous one, but it was important to San Antonio. The existing drainage system was so poor that large sections of the city, particularly the poorer neighborhoods, suffered severe flooding after heavy rainstorms. By moving to rectify this situation, Cisneros was working to improve health and environmental conditions within San Antonio as well as the lives of the city's Mexican Americans.

At the same time, Cisneros worked hard to create a policy of inclusiveness, just as he had during his tenure on the city council. He had no intention of being labeled a "Mexican" mayor or a "Hispanic" spokesman. Cisneros wanted the city's whites, blacks, Asians, and American Indians to be as comfortable with his leadership as were the members of the Mexican community, and he wanted the business community to understand that he was seeking to improve the city as a whole.

As mayor, Cisneros stepped up his efforts to bring businesses and tourists to San Antonio. Among the main points of his program were plans to create an industrial park for high-technology industries; to build a stadium that would bring a professional football team to the city; to erect a Sea World amusement park; and to complete River Walk, a major complex of

At a ceremony in the White House, Cisneros (far left) is sworn in as a member of the National Bipartisan Commission on Central America. Strongly disagreeing with the Reagan administration's hard-line policies in Central America, Cisneros did his best to convince the 11 other commission members that a more enlightened approach to the region was needed.

shops, malls, offices, parks, and restaurants along the San Antonio River. Though not everyone in San Antonio was in favor of all of Cisneros's proposals, the voters agreed almost unanimously that their new mayor was taking the right approach to revitalizing the city. When Cisneros sought a second term in 1983, he was reelected with an almost incredible 94.2 percent of the vote.

Cisneros's performance in San Antonio was attracting nationwide attention. In the summer of 1983, President Ronald Reagan appointed Cisneros to his 12-member National Bipartisan Commission on Central America. Cisneros was flattered by the president's attention, but he was also troubled by it. He certainly did not support the highly conservative Reagan administration's policies on Central America, and he was reluctant to do anything that would help to legitimize those policies. Nevertheless, Cisneros knew that he would have more influence as a member of the commission than he would as an outside critic, so he accepted the appointment.

The main issue in Reagan's Central American policy at the time was the nation of Nicaragua, where the left-wing Sandinista government was being challenged by right-wing forces known as the contras. The Reagan administration claimed that the Sandinistas, supported by the Communist regimes of the Soviet Union and Cuba, were encouraging unrest and revolution in other Central American countries. The United States was therefore giving aid to the contras, and Reagan did not rule out the possibility of direct U.S. military action.

The Bipartisan Commission was chaired by former secretary of state Henry Kissinger. Cisneros came to respect Kissinger's intellect, if not his political orientation. The commission, although bipartisan (made up of both Republicans and Democrats) clearly supported the Reagan administration's policies. Cisneros attempted to explain to the other members of the commission that poverty and social injustice in Central America was a greater threat than communism. He argued that U.S. economic aid, rather than military intervention, would be more helpful to the people of Central America in the long run and bring about greater influence for the United States. His arguments generally fell on deaf ears.

Serving on the commission was thus a frustrating experience for Cisneros, but it provided him with his first real experience in international affairs. This experience would be extremely valuable if he chose to run for national office. He also received national exposure; during his months of service, Cisneros was covered frequently and favorably in the news media. His name had not quite become a household word, but political

Henry and Mary Alice Cisneros, along with their daughters, Teresa (left) and Mercedes, join Walter and Joan Mondale in North Oaks, Minnesota, on July 4, 1984. Though Mondale interviewed Cisneros for the vice-presidential spot on the Democratic ticket, he had already decided to choose New York congresswoman Geraldine Ferraro.

analysts were portraying him more and more as a rising star in the Democratic party.

In 1984, Cisneros's new celebrity status led to an interesting opportunity. Walter Mondale, the Democratic presidential nominee in the 1984 election, had been impressed with Cisneros for a long time. He was even more impressed after Cisneros helped to shore up Mondale's support in the Democratic primary election in Texas. Even though he had the nomination in his pocket before the Democratic convention began, Mondale knew that he was in very big trouble. Reagan's popularity was so high in the summer of 1984 that only a devastating mistake on the president's

part would change the outcome of the election. Still, Mondale had one card left to play. He thought that if he selected a vice-presidential running mate who was a woman or a member of a minority group—or both—he might stand a better chance against Reagan. Mondale saw little risk in this plan; even if he lost the election, as most people expected him to do, he would have made a gesture toward Democratic party unity that could help the Democrats regain the White House at some point in the future. He would also be making history: no major party had ever nominated a woman or a Hispanic or an African American for either the presidency or vice-presidency.

As the Democratic National Cenvention approached, Mondale interviewed potential running mates at his home in Minnesota and proclaimed loudly to the press that every single one of them was actually being considered for the job. Cisneros arrived for his interview with his wife and two daughters; he wanted Teresa and Mercedes to remember the day's events. He knew perfectly well that he had no chance of getting the nod, whatever Mondale told the press. Just 37 years old, Cisneros was barely old enough to serve as vice-president—the Constitution requires a minimum age of 35. He was far too young to be seriously considered, and besides, both he and Mondale knew that the Hispanic vote was safely Democratic. There was nothing to be gained at the polls by having Cisneros on the ticket. Mondale had in fact already decided on a female running mate, hoping to lure Republican and independent women voters. Mondale knew that many women were outraged by the Reagan administration's campaign against abortion rights, and he felt that if he had a woman on the ticket he could bring that controversy to the forefront of the campaign. It was a desperate move, but by that time Mondale was a desperate candidate.

Not being chosen for the 1984 Democratic ticket was politically one of the best things that ever happened to Cisneros. Mondale and his running mate, Congresswoman Geraldine Ferraro of New York City, were crushed by President Reagan and Vice-President George Bush, in the worst electoral vote defeat in Democratic party history. Reagan carried 49 out of 50 states, leaving only Mondale's home state of Min-

Cisneros addresses the 1984 Democratic National Convention, stressing the need for aid to the nation's cities. At the age of 37, San Antonio's mayor had emerged as an appealing figure in the Democratic party, one who combined social idealism with a hardheaded view of economic policy.

nesota, along with the District of Columbia, to the Democrats.

Reagan's landslide victory ended Mondale's political career and also signaled the death of the New Deal wing of the Democratic party, which had first come to power during the 1930s under the leadership of President Franklin D. Roosevelt. Whereas the New Dealers had relied on large-scale government action to tackle social problems, Cisneros was part of a different generation of Democrats—those who were still concerned about reform but envisioned a greater role for private enterprise in moving the nation forward.

If Cisneros had joined Mondale's ticket, his political career might have been over, too. Historically, losing vice-presidential candidates have faded quickly from the political landscape. By remaining on the sidelines, Cisneros emerged from the 1984 election campaign as a winner. The fact that he had been interviewed for the vice-presidential slot at such a young age added to his growing national prestige, and political observers around the country began to talk about him as someone who might be a presidential candidate sometime in the future.

Cisneros was easily reelected mayor of San Antonio in 1985, for a third term, and then reelected again in 1987. In 1985 he was also elected president of the National League of Cities, the organization that had given him his first full-time job. Before Cisneros completed his fourth term in office, however, two major upheavals in his personal life threatened to wreck his political career for good.

Two months after Henry was elected to his fourth term as mayor, Mary Alice Cisneros gave birth to the couple's third child and first son, John Paul. The baby was born prematurely, however, and the doctors soon discovered that he had a serious and possibly fatal heart disorder. Faced with John Paul's illness, Cisneros

John Paul Cisneros visits with his father in the mayor's office in 1986. John Paul's heart ailment was one of the factors influencing Cisneros to retire from public life the following year.

began to question some of the choices he had made; he started to wonder if the strenuous life of a politician was really what he wanted. Cisneros knew that it would be a blessing if John Paul was ever able to live a normal life—if he lived at all. Cisneros did not want to miss precious moments with his son, especially if those moments would be limited to a few short years.

During his fourth term, Cisneros also became involved in an extramarital affair with a campaign aide, and the affair became public knowledge in San Antonio. With the embarrassment of a public scandal added to their concern over their son's medical condition, Henry and Mary Alice Cisneros endured a painful period of soul searching. In the end, they decided that they wanted to save their marriage and keep their family together. Having made this decision, Cisneros decided that he could not continue to give the people of San Antonio the sort of leadership to which they had become accustomed. Despite an emotional outpouring of support, and the pleas of many that he remain in office, Cisneros did not seek a fifth term as mayor.

After 12 years of public life, Cisneros went into business for himself, establishing the Cisneros Asset Management Group, a financial services firm. However, he did not withdraw from the public eye or from community service. For three years, he was the host of "Texans," a one-hour television show that aired every three months, and of "Adelante," a national radio program produced in Spanish. He also served as deputy chairman of the Federal Reserve Bank of Dallas, as chairman of the National Civic League, and as a board member of the Rockefeller Foundation, a leading charitable trust. Cisneros was also highly active in the planning and construction of the Alamodome, a new sports and entertainment complex in downtown San Antonio.

Interviewed by Earl Shorris in his well-appointed offices near the River Walk complex he had pioneered, Cisneros admitted that financial pressures—medical bills for his son, tuition fees for his daughters—had been part of his decision to leave office. He also confessed that the stresses of being a minority politician had begun to wear on him:

> It's very difficult in our society to live in the middle.... As much as you might try to represent the interests of the Hispanic community, you find yourself up against a system where you constantly have to compromise, because it's not possible to drive through a system of school finance that gives the kind of money that needs to be going into minority districts. Because you don't have the array of power in Texas yet to be able to do that. . . . You are, by definition, an instrument of compromise . . . between those who have the luxury of being ideologically

pure—on the left—and at the same time, not a believer in the ideology of the right, of business, of power. And so the person ends up a bridge, but a bridge takes a lot of wear and tear. Bridges are to be trampled upon, trampled across, I should say. And so it takes a very strong sense of self, of mission, and of stamina, to play that role.

Those who concluded from such remarks that Cisneros himself no longer had the will or the energy to continue the fight did not truly understand him. His dedication to public service had not been at all diminished, and his desire to return to politics became stronger as his son's health improved and as he and Mary Alice resolved their difficulties. During the same period of time, the Democratic party was changing as well, and the stage was being set for the political comeback of Henry Cisneros.

CHAPTER

EIGHT

RETURN TO
WASHINGTON

In five out of six presidential elections between 1968 and 1988, the Republican candidate was victorious. The only Democrat elected during that time was former Georgia governor Jimmy Carter, who occupied the White House from 1976 to 1980, when he was defeated by Ronald Reagan. In 1992, Americans chose another Democratic southern governor, Bill Clinton of Arkansas, to be the nation's chief executive. For the first time in a dozen years, the Democrats were firmly in control of the government.

Cisneros had been instrumental in helping Clinton win the presidency, even though the Republican candidate, President George Bush, had carried the state of Texas. Democratic campaigners such as Cisneros had helped to keep the election close in Texas. They had forced the Republicans to expend valuable resources in order to keep Texas in their column, thus weakening their efforts in other states.

During the campaign, Clinton made it clear that he intended to appoint a large number of women, blacks, and Latinos to important positions in his administration. Cisneros never needed any special consideration based on his ethnicity, however. There were very few people in the United States of any race or ethnicity who possessed Cisneros's educational and professional credentials, as well as his political experi-

Cisneros takes part in a 1992 California campaign rally with Democratic presidential candidate Bill Clinton and U.S. Senate candidate Barbara Boxer. Because Cisneros's support was a great help to Clinton in California and the Southwest, it was no surprise when the new president chose the former San Antonio mayor to serve in his cabinet.

97

ence. Long before the votes were tallied, Democratic insiders were asking not whether Cisneros would play a part in a Clinton administration but rather which specific cabinet post he would fill.

The president's cabinet consists of a number of high officials who advise the president and serve as the chief executives of various government agencies, such as the Department of State and the Department of Justice. After he was elected in 1992, Bill Clinton named Cisneros secretary of housing and urban development—a fairly new cabinet position that had been created by Lyndon B. Johnson in 1966, just two years before Cisneros started working for the Johnson administration in the Model Cities program.

During much of its recent history, the Department of Housing and Urban Development had been led by

During a tour of public housing in Flint, Michigan, in February 1993, Cisneros exchanges ideas with Michigan senator Don Riegle (foreground) and other government officials. As secretary of housing and urban development, Cisneros combined hands-on political experience with a broad knowledge of urban problems.

a series of colorless and seemingly uncaring bureau-crats. There had been one exception—the man who had filled the position immediately before Cisneros. Jack Kemp, a former quarterback with the Buffalo Bills, had been appointed by President Bush and had come to the job as a conservative. But Kemp was also a very hard worker and a creative, open-minded man who had a sincere desire to help the poor people of the nation. Kemp proved to be a big (and unwelcome) surprise to his party, as he ventured forth into housing projects and tried to determine the needs of the people who lived in them. Though he was increasingly isolated within the conservative Bush administration, Kemp became as popular with some of the nation's poor as he had been with the football fans in Buffalo years before.

Kemp helped to prepare the way for Cisneros, who came to HUD with pent-up energy that got him into his office at 7:00 A.M. every morning. He also brought a vision of activism that reached far beyond the bureaucracy of housing. "HUD must be an advocate for America's cities and communities," he announced to the press. "HUD must also talk truth to the country about issues of racism, what racism has meant to Americans. We must talk truth about the creation of the new American social contract in an era of diversity."

Part of that social contract, in Cisneros's view, was equality in housing. Cisneros stated his belief that HUD should have the authority to deny federal funds to any community refusing to integrate public housing, and he followed up on that conviction with swift personal action in the Vidor Village controversy in 1993.

Cisneros also tackled one of America's most saddening and shameful problems—the homeless people filling the streets of the nation's cities. "Helping the homeless is our number one priority," he announced. Making a tour of Washington's streets and shelters in January 1993, he was appalled at what he found. "An African-American woman, eight months pregnant, sleeping on the lawn of the Justice Department!" he exclaimed to reporters. "Five veterans, sleeping on a heat grate for warmth. Incredible things—veterans!" Cisneros immediately proposed spending more than $100 million for programs to house the homeless and train them for jobs, and he said he would ask the president to sign an order opening underused military bases to homeless groups.

As he developed his ideas further, Cisneros tried to shift the government's approach away from providing only emergency housing. Announcing a pilot program in Washington called the D.C. Homeless Initiative, he focused on longer-term social services, substance-abuse treatment, and job training. Cisneros's plan also called for creating permanent housing for the homeless, a more expensive solution than emergency shelters at first glance, but a much more economical, and humane, alternative in the long term. Cisneros's approach was comprehensive, innovative, and fundamentally conservative. His plan for helping the homeless clearly illustrated the new Democratic philosophy—providing government aid that was conditioned upon individual responsibility.

Cisneros continued to push for his programs during his first year in office, even though it became clear that many of the "new Democrats" were not anxious to embrace the homeless or any other group of people who did not represent a large, influential special interest group or block of voters. Cisneros himself knew that making the homeless his highest priority would not add up to a lot of votes in any future campaign, but he was determined to go on with his efforts. "I'm here because I think the country's in trouble," he said.

Cisneros talks with two young residents of Chicago's Cabrini-Green Housing Project in June 1993. Upon taking office, Cisneros declared, "HUD must be an advocate for America's cities and communities. . . . HUD must also talk truth to the country about issues of racism."

"We ought not to waste time talking about anything but the truth, anything but the core reality."

Cisneros did not hesitate to acknowledge HUD's past failings. Referring to the horrendous and unlivable conditions of many of the nation's housing projects, Cisneros told a U.S. Senate committee that "HUD's management of its own inventory has been abysmal" and admitted that the department had "exacerbated the declining quality of life in America." These were bold words for a cabinet member to use when speaking of his own department, but blunt talk was in keeping with Cisneros's style.

He was no less forthright when talking of his own personal difficulties. Whereas most political figures do whatever possible to suppress anything that reflects badly on their public image, Cisneros spoke openly about the scandal that had, in part, caused him to step aside as mayor of San Antonio. "I haven't lied to the public about anything," he told a reporter from the New York *Daily News.* "I just don't do it. It's kind of a sacred trust. . . . I guess I feel that as distasteful and painful as the evolution of journalism is, and where this whole kind of reporting [about politicians' private lives] has gone, in the final analysis it's probably the best thing. We can learn about people in all their dimensions, and we can make judgments about people and all of their flaws and foibles and not reward the person who's able to create the best cardboard cutout image of the perfect person."

As he settled into his new job, Cisneros began to look beyond the specific problem of housing to the condition of the nation's cities as a whole, especially the link between racism and poverty. In an address to the National Urban League, Cisneros stated, "We know that one of the barriers to economic advancement for many blacks is that they do not live where the jobs are and are discriminated against when seeking housing in many localities." Referring to the 1992 Los Angeles riots, Cisneros asked his listeners at the Progressive Policy Institute conference, "Why are our cities smoldering? Well, perhaps it's a matter of isolation. Our cities and neighborhoods have become more geographically segregated by race, class and ethnicity." At a later date, he explained to an interviewer: "There has been a disintegration of social order in our cities, as life has become more untenable. It's partly due to a lack of jobs and partly due to changing economic functions. Jobs no longer match the skills that people have."

Cisneros did not, however, abandon his original priorities. As a cold wave descended on the nation's capital in November 1993, Cisneros was outraged to learn that a 43-year-old homeless woman, Yetta M. Adams, had frozen to death at a bus stop across the street from the HUD offices. Speaking at Adams's funeral, Cisneros repeated his call for aid to the homeless. "On the morning of November 29, an entire nation was called to conscience," he declared. "An entire country learned of a lady who died on the streets of the city. She said to all Americans, 'Something is not right.' She made it clear to those of us in government that we must do better." Cisneros responded to Adams's death by pledging an immediate expenditure of $250,000 to provide more beds in the city's shelters and upgrade a telephone hotline providing social service information for the homeless.

In the summer of 1993, Cisneros was reminded again of how fragile life can be even for those who have jobs and homes. His son, John Paul, had to undergo another heart operation, fortunately with a successful outcome. "Life can take some strange turns," Cisneros told an interviewer. "I can only say that I am grateful for the blessings I have."

At the age of 46, Cisneros certainly appeared to have many blessings and a bright political future. He ranked as the most prominent Mexican American in contemporary government and perhaps the most prominent in U.S. history, along with fellow Texan Henry B. Gonzalez, the chairman of the powerful Banking Committee of the U.S. House of Representatives. Cisneros is one of a handful of major Hispanic political leaders, but that will surely change in the near future—the Hispanic population is the fastest growing segment of the U.S. population.

"I do not have a national constituency, because I am not an elected official," Cisneros explained to an interviewer. "But I do feel a connection to Latinos all over the country." When pressed about the future of Latinos in the Democratic party and the possibility of their turning more toward the Republican party, Cisneros was emphatic. "It won't happen. Republicans have a hard time winning Latinos. It's a young population, and the people need government services. La-

Cisneros poses for a family portrait with his wife, children, and parents, in December 1993. Completing his first full year as a cabinet official, Cisneros was being widely discussed as a possible presidential candidate at some point in the future.

tinos are socially conservative in most ways. But economically, they are and will remain liberal."

Cisneros was not eager to discuss his own political future. When asked about the possibility of seeking the nation's highest office, he said, "I really have no ambition to seek the presidency." But it is hard to believe that a leader with Cisneros's intelligence, education, and abilities will depart from the national scene in the near future. He could be given a more powerful role within the Clinton administration, such as secretary of state or secretary of the Treasury. After leaving Washington, he could decide to run for the governorship of Texas or for one of the state's two seats in the U.S. Senate. Sometime around the beginning of the 21st century, he may finally be ready to make a run for the White House. Whatever he decides, he will have an impact on the nation and on the political scene. Henry Cisneros has never lost an election, and he has no intention of ever doing so.

CHRONOLOGY

1947   Born Henry Gabriel Cisneros in San Antonio, Texas, on June 11

1964   Enrolls at Texas A & M University

1968   Receives B.A. from Texas A & M; begins work with Model Cities program in San Antonio

1969   Appointed assistant director of Model Cities program in San Antonio; earns master's degree in urban and regional planning from Texas A & M; marries Mary Alice Pérez

1970   Moves to Washington, D.C., to study at George Washington University

1971   Selected as a White House Fellow

1973   Awarded master's degree in public administration from John F. Kennedy School of Government, Harvard University; receives Ph.D. in public administration from George Washington University

1975   Elected to San Antonio City Council for first of three two-year terms

1981   Elected mayor of San Antonio

1989   Decides not to seek a fifth term as mayor, citing family responsibilities; forms Cisneros Asset Management

1992   Appointed secretary of housing and urban development in Clinton administration

FURTHER READING

Bernotas, Bob. *The Department of Housing and Urban Development.* New York: Chelsea House, 1991.

Cisneros, Henry G. *Interwoven Destinies: Cities and the Nation.* New York: Norton, 1993.

Cockcroft, James D. *Outlaws in the Promised Land: Mexican Immigrant Workers and America's Future.* New York: Grove Press, 1986.

Cronon, William, et al. *Under an Open Sky: Rethinking America's Western Past.* New York: Norton, 1992.

DeParle, Jason. "Housing Secretary is Suddenly Assertive on Aiding Homeless." *New York Times,* January 30, 1993.

Diehl, Kemper, and Jan Jarboe. *Cisneros: Portrait of a New American.* San Antonio: Corona, 1984.

Garcia, Mario T. *Mexican Americans.* New Haven: Yale University Press, 1989.

Marshall, Will, and Martin Schram. *Mandate for Change.* Berkeley, CA: The Progressive Policy Institute, 1993.

Milligan, Susan. "HUD Boss Out to Raise Roof." *New York Daily News,* April 11, 1993.

Montejano, David. *Anglos and Mexicans in the Making of Texas, 1836–1986.* Austin: University of Texas Press, 1987.

Osborne, David, and Ted Gaebler. *Reinventing Government.* New York: Plume/Penguin, 1992.

Riding, Alan. *Distant Neighbors: A Portrait of the Mexicans.* New York: Vintage, 1984.

Shorris, Earl. *Latinos: A Biography of the People.* New York: Norton, 1992.

Weber, David J. *The Spanish Frontier in North America.* New Haven: Yale University Press, 1992.

INDEX

CHRISTOPHER HENRY is a New York attorney in private practice who represents business and professional clients worldwide. He is the author of two books about U.S. immigration law as well as numerous other works. His books for young readers include *Ben Nighthorse Campbell* in Chelsea Houses's NORTH AMERICAN INDIANS OF ACHIEVEMENT series and *Julian Bond* in the Chelsea House BLACK AMERICANS OF ACHIEVEMENT series. Henry has also chronicled the lives of Chief Justice William H. Rehnquist and Associate Justice Ruth Bader Ginsburg in Chelsea House's *Justices of the United States Supreme Court, 1789–1994*. Since 1990, Henry has been accredited as a delegate to the United Nations, where he represents the Brehon Law Society, an association of attorneys and jurists concerned with human rights and the administration of justice in Northern Ireland.

RODOLFO CARDONA is professor of Spanish and comparative literature at Boston University. A renowned scholar, he has written many works of criticism, including *Ramón, a Study of Gómez de la Serna and His Works* and *Visión del esperpento: Teoría y práctica del esperpento en Valle-Inclán*. Born in San José, Costa Rica, he earned his B.A. and M.A. from Louisiana State University and received a Ph.D. from the University of Washington. He has taught at Case Western Reserve University, the University of Pittsburgh, the University of Texas at Austin, the University of New Mexico, and Harvard University.

JAMES COCKCROFT is currently a visiting professor of Latin American and Caribbean studies at the State University of New York at Albany. A three-time Fulbright scholar, he earned a Ph.D. from Stanford University and has taught at the University of Massachusetts, the University of Vermont, and the University of Connecticut. He is the author or coauthor of numerous books on Latin American subjects, including *Neighbors in Turmoil: Latin America, The Hispanic Experience in the United States: Contemporary Issues and Perspectives,* and *Outlaws in the Promised Land: Mexican Immigrant Workers and America's Future.*

PICTURE CREDITS